AN

EPITOME

OF THE

HISTORY OF PHILOSOPHY.

BEING

THE WORK ADOPTED BY THE UNIVERSITY OF FRANCE
FOR INSTRUCTION IN THE COLLEGES AND
HIGH SCHOOLS.

TRANSLATED FROM THE FRENCH,

WITH

ADDITIONS, AND A CONTINUATION OF THE HISTORY
FROM THE TIME OF REID TO THE
PRESENT DAY.

BY C. S. HENRY, D.D.,
PROFESSOR OF PHILOSOPHY AND HISTORY IN THE UNIVERSITY
OF THE CITY OF NEW-YORK.

IN TWO VOLUMES.

VOL. II.

NEW YORK:
HARPER & BROTHERS, PUBLISHERS,
FRANKLIN SQUARE.
1856.

CONTENTS

OF

THE SECOND VOLUME.

FIFTH PERIOD.

MODERN PHILOSOPHY.

APPENDIX.

SKETCH OF THE HISTORY OF PHILOSOPHY FROM REID TO THE PRESENT TIME.

ENGLISH PHILOSOPHY IN THE CLOSE OF THE EIGHTEENTH CENTURY.

PHILOSOPHY IN THE NINETEENTH CENTURY.

ENGLISH PHILOSOPHY.

GERMAN PHILOSOPHY IN THE NINETEENTH CENTURY.

FRENCH PHILOSOPHY IN THE NINETEENTH CENTURY.

SENSUAL SCHOOL.

THEOLOGICAL SPIRITUALISM.

RATIONAL PSYCHOLOGISTS, OR ECLECTIC SCHOOL.

AN EPITOME

OF THE

HISTORY OF PHILOSOPHY.

FIFTH PERIOD.

MODERN PHILOSOPHY

We here distinguish two phases. To the first belong the systems resulting from a philosophical impulse communicated anterior to that determined by the great schools founded by Bacon, Descartes, and Leibnitz. The second phase comprehends the systems more or less directly connected with the influence exercised by those three great reformers of philosophy.

FIRST PHASE.

The fifteenth and sixteenth centuries produced a multitude of writings relating to philosophy. They may be divided into several classes.

1. Works which consist chiefly of commentaries upon the books of the ancient philosophers. In this class belong the writings of many Greek authors who took refuge in Italy on the downfall of the Lower Empire, as Gemisthius Pletho, Theodore Gaza, George Trebizond, Cardinal Bessarion; many of these commentaries contain discussions respecting the pre-eminence of Plàtonism above Aristotelianism.

2. Works produced by the controversy between

the Humanists against the schoolmen. This controversy was, however, rather literary than philosophical. The Humanists, enthusiastic admirers of Greek and Roman literature, more frequently attacked the forms than the substance of scholasticism. These quarrels belong, nevertheless, to the history of philosophy, because all the blows struck at the scholastic systems had their effect in calling forth a new philosophy. In this conflict were particularly distinguished in Italy Hermolaus Barbarus and Angelo Politian; in Germany, Ulrich de Hutten and Erasmus.

3. Works that united, either with commentaries or with philological explanations, some new conceptions, which, however, did not constitute philosophical systems. Here belong the writings of Marcellus Ficinus, a Florentine noticeable for his Platonism, as also those of John Picus of Mirandola in Italy, and of Reuchlin in Germany, who endeavoured to revive cabalistic ideas under a Christian form.

The history of this epoch recites still many other writers who formed either apologists or adversaries of the principal doctrines of the Greek schools.

We shall not go into any details respecting the different works which we have just indicated; we shall occupy ourselves solely with such philosophical conceptions as present the characteristics of systems properly speaking. They are divided into two classes: ontological systems, which have for their object the explanation of things; and logical systems, which relate either to the condition or to the processes of human reason.

I. ONTOLOGICAL SYSTEMS.

We divide these, according to their different relations to the question concerning the origin of things, into theistical, pantheistic, and atheistic systems, remarking, however, that this classification should be combined with another division determined by the different points of view taken in regard to the origin and nature of human knowledge.

Theistical Systems.

NICHOLAS DE CUSA.

Born in the diocese of Treves in 1401. He died in Italy in the year 1464. The alliance of metaphysics and mathematics greatly engaged his mind. He devoted himself also to physical speculations, and preluded the Copernican system, by renewing the hypothesis of Pythagoras respecting the motion of the earth. In many respects he opened a different route from that which the schoolmen had travelled over, by attempting to construct a philosophy that exhibits a mixture of Pythagorean ideas with new conceptions, remarkable for their originality and often for their profoundness.

We signalize the following points: 1. Philosophy may be divided into two orders: transcendental science, whose object is the primitive, absolute, infinite unity; and inferior science, which has multiplicity for its object.

2. The absolute unity is incomprehensible in itself; it can be known only by symbols. Transcendental science, as soon as it makes any pretension of being a direct knowledge, is full of uncertainties. [These ideas have some analogy with the principles developed by Kant.]

3. From the primal unity proceeded all beings, which would be as its fractions, if such a term could be applied to the indivisible unity.

4. The phenomena of nature correspond to math-

ematics. [This principle has been consecrated by the theories of Newton.]

5. Human reason, like nature, does not operate but by means of ideas of number, ideas which are its constitutive form.

6. Humanity aspires after unity or perfection, without wishing to lose its own proper nature. If we suppose an unlimited progress, man will be forever looking and reaching towards a higher perfection, and will never obtain the goal which he seeks. If this progress be limited, the innate desire of humanity will be still farther from being satisfied. We cannot, therefore, conceive that this perfection can be attained unless so far as the supreme perfection, God, shall unite himself to human nature. "Humanity," says Nicholas de Cusa, "that by which all men are men, is one, and the movement of my human nature has for its object the attainment of God in man."

Theosophy.

PARACELSUS. VAN HELMONT.

The physician Bombast de Hohenheim, born at Einsiedlen, in Switzerland, in 1493, known by the name of Theophrastus Paracelsus, distinguished himself by his opposition to the scholastic medical science. He travelled throughout Europe, and probably, also, many countries of the East. Governed by an ardent imagination, he devoted himself to alchymy. He died in 1541, at Salzburg.

Paracelsus took, as the basis of his physical speculations, theosophy; that is, a direct communication of the soul with God by means of illumination.

The soul, resembling God, contains in its own depths all truth that man can know; it is full of sciences, but all these notions, all these divine characters are veiled or obscured. Consequently, it is not by the senses, by books, by reasoning, by factitious intelligence, that man can arrive at science ; it is by retiring within himself, by withdrawing into the essential intelligence which is in the depths of his nature : there he perceives the truth, not actively, but passively, by divine illumination, of which purity of heart is the condition, and prayer the means.

It is there that he recognises the plan of creation to be one, and, consequently, that the universe, the great world, is made after the same model as man, or the little world, which is as its child. Man is a hidden world.

God, who is life, has diffused life everywhere ; all parts of the universe are full of souls, who, however, have not been gifted with intelligence, the privilege of man created in the image of God. Souls are enveloped in bodies or matter, which is in itself a dark and dead thing : between souls and bodies exists the spirit, a sort of fluid, which is the physical means of the universal life. The soul, the fluid, the body : such is the trinity of nature, which in some respects is a counterpart of the divine Trinity.

In the same way man contains in himself three principles, three worlds, three heavens : the soul, by which he communicates with God, or the archetypal world ; the material body, which puts him in connexion with the elementary world ; and the spiritual body, which, being formed of ethereal fluid, is in perpetual communication with the angelic-astral world. This spiritual body, the fine envelope of the soul, reminds one of the subtile person of the Sankhya philosophy.

The triple nature of man and the triple nature of the world being identical, there exists in man a force of attraction by which he aspires to the life of the world. He possesses at first a magnetic power which draws from the elements the nourishment of his flesh and blood. There is also in him a superior magnetism, which attracts the spiritual fluid, the principle of sensations and of worldly wisdom; and this magnetism is itself subordinated to the aspiration by which the soul is nourished from God. But, at the same time that he attracts all the forces of nature, man improves them in himself, and recalls them all to God, the universal centre. Thus the world is a flux and reflux of the divine life by means of man.

Paracelsus combined with these ideas a multitude of physical speculations, more or less fantastic, which resulted in theurgy and magic.

Van Helmont, originally of Brussels, was born in 1577, and died in 1664. He adopted the method and many of the ideas of Paracelsus. He criticised the logical methods in order to demonstrate their insufficiency, and to substitute another process. The knowledge of the relation which exists between the terms of a syllogism exist in our minds prior to the conclusion; it follows, therefore, that logic is nothing but a means of recapitulating anterior notions, which has no other use than to facilitate the exposition of ideas on the part of a speaker, and the recollection of them on the part of the hearer. All true science is therefore independent of demonstration, and can be acquired only by pure intuition. Van Helmont sought to discover the internal cause of phenomena, which he called *archeus* (αρχη), and he decided it to consist in the union of spirit, of the vital breath, with the seminal image, or internal type of each being. Many of his ideas, as well as those of Paracelsus, are analogous to the modern theories of magnetism. He connected, like the Swiss philosopher, physical speculations with an ecstatic contemplation of the divine unity, to which one could elevate himself only by that state of abstraction, passivity, self-annihilation, which formed the old dream of the Hindu philosophy.

To these theosophists should be added Jacob Boehme, whose philosophy has its partisans at this day in Germany.

Theosophy divided itself into two branches. While in Germany and Belgium it produced, by means of illumination, a physical philosophy, it was applied in Spain and Italy to the moral world, and produced in that Quietism. Molines made true virtue, perfect piety, to consist in the annihilation of all will, just as Paracelsus and Van Helmont had made true science to depend upon the annihilation of every intellectual operation.

Naturalism.

TELESIO.

WHILE Paracelsus derived the science of nature from theosophy, Telesio, born in the kingdom of Naples in 1508, attempted to convert that science into speculations purely physical, which admit God as the creator, but as to the rest, allow no notion of his intervention in the theory of the world. We shall meet presently, in the physical part of the system of Campanella, the ideas of Telesio concerning the two constituent principles of nature and the universal diffusion of the faculty of feeling.

The speculations of Patrizzi, born in 1529, are something intermediate between the philosophy of Paracelsus and that of Telesio. They are a mixture of mysticism and naturalism.

II.—

CAMPANELLA.

Thomas Campanella was born at a town in Calabria in 1568. He entered the order of the Dominicans. He suffered greatly from the persecutions of his enemies, and at last took refuge in France under the protection of Cardinal Richelieu. He died in 1639, at Paris, in a convent of his order.

Campanella formed a theory of human knowledge and a logic. He reduced the intelligence to the faculty of feeling, that is, of perceiving the modifications of our own being; thought is nothing but the generalization of various perceptions, and sentiment is their collective whole. His logic, which differs on many points from the logic of Aristotle, corresponds to his principles concerning the source of the intelligence. It is an intellectual instrument, appropriated particularly to the study of nature.

Campanella, unfaithful therein to his theory of knowledge, rests all his speculations upon the basis of a vast metaphysics. All creatures are composed of being and non-being; and being in its transcendent composition is constituted by power, wisdom, and love, which have for their object essence, truth, and goodness; as non-being is weakness, ignorance, and hatred. These three primordial qualities subsist originally in the Supreme Being; are there united, according to an incomprehensible simplicity, without any mixture of non-being; they are one, though distinct. This being, in drawing all things from non-being, transfers his inexhaustible ideas into matter, under the condition of time, the image of eternity, and upon the basis of space, which has its solidity in God, and he communicates to finite beings the three qualities which become the principles of the universe under the triple law of necessity, of Providence, and of harmony. With this metaphysics as the centre of all the speculations of Campanella, are co-ordinated a physical philosophy, a physiological philosophy, and a social or political philosophy.

In his physical philosophy he treats of the universe in as far as it is an aggregate of material phenomena. These phenomena are developed in space and in time, which are at once something real and something relative. Space, taken in itself, is an incorporeal, immutable substance, the receptacle of bodies; but every measure of space, everything which we designate by the terms high and low, is relative to ourselves. Time in itself is the duration of the essence of things; relative to us it is number in motion. Matter, situated in time and space, is not constructed, but fitted for construction, which is effected by two universal agents, heat and cold. Heat, which volatilizes, formed heaven, which is composed of a delicate matter; cold formed the earth by condensing matter. The celestial element, the seat of heat, and the terrestrial element, the seat of cold, produce by combination all phenomena. Light and heat are identical; they are one and the same agent, which is heat in relation to the touch, light in relation to the sight. In relation to the touch, cold should be night. All colours are a compound of darkness and light, of black and white, for pure white is light itself. Such are the general principles of the physics of Campanella: we cannot follow him in the numerous applications he has made, or, rather, sought to make, of them.

His physiology, which considers beings so far as having life, turns upon an induction by which he concludes from man to the universe. He distinguishes in man a triple life, corresponding to a triple substance: the intelligence, which is the highest part of the soul; the spirit, the vehicle of intelligence, the seat of the sensations, and the principle of the appetites; and, lastly, the body, the vehicle and organ of the intelligence and of the spirit. But as all beings, even those which are called brutes, tend to their preservation by motions as well arranged for this end as the motions of the human organization are to its preservation, Campanella concludes that all beings are endowed with instincts, and endowed also, like man, with the faculty of feeling, which is developed in nature in various degrees. Still farther, if man, besides spirit, possesses an immortal intelligence, *à fortiori*, the world, which is the most perfect of beings, ought to possess not only a sentient spirit, but also an intelligent soul, which presides over its totality. What though the world have neither eyes, nor ears, nor hands, nor feet; its intelligent substance, as well as its sentient substance, has superior organs: the expansive forces are its hands, the stars are its eyes, and it may be conjectured that the rays which the stars send forth from one to the other are a high language by which they mutually communicate their thoughts. Here Campanella enters upon astrology, which occupies a large place in his speculations.

Social or political philosophy has for its object the reformation of humanity; and this reformation, if it were complete, would consist in re-establishing the integrity and harmony of power, wisdom, and love, the three primordial qualities, which the passions of man have corrupted or put at variance. In his book entitled *Of the City of the Sun*, Campanella has traced the plan of a typical society. It is ruled by a supreme chief, who represents God, who has three ministers, presiding, the one over the physical force, the other over the propagation of science and wisdom, and the third over social union and the intercourse of life. But, singularly enough, this treatise contains nearly all the bases of St. Simonianism: community of goods and wives, the destruction of family and domestic relations, the transformation of domestic service into public functions, and the public authority, which consists solely in directing the labourers, exercised in each degree of the hierarchy by one man and one woman. Campanella, however, presented this typical society, so far as it implied the destruction of marriage and all the immoral consequences resulting therefrom, only as something intermediate between the degradation of heathen society and the social perfection of which Christianity is the principle.

Pantheism.

JORDANO BRUNO.

About the commencement of the sixteenth century, Pomponatius, an Italian, had borrowed from the philosophy of Averroes many principles incompatible with the Catholic faith; and some time afterward Jerome Cardan, of Pavia, who died in 1576, had equally infringed upon orthodoxy by his fantastic opinions. But greater errors were soon produced. A pantheistic system, the precursor of Spinoza's, appeared in the writings of Jordano Bruno, born at Nola, in the kingdom of Naples, about the middle of the sixteenth century. After having embraced the religious life in a convent of the Dominicans, he fled to Geneva, where he made a profession of Calvinism. He afterward travelled in France, England, and Germany. He returned to Italy, when he was arrested and taken to Rome, where he was condemned and burned to death in 1600.

The system of Jordano Bruno has been interpreted

in various ways. The following is our conception of it in its fundamental principles, as we gather it by combining various principles scattered through his writings:

Nothing exists which is not one; for everything which is not one is, in as far as it is multiple, only a compound, and every composition is only an aggregate of relations, and not a reality. Unity is therefore being, and being is reality. Unless we admit that everything is relative, an opinion repugnant to human reason, which tends to the absolute, we must acknowledge an absolute unity, without parts without limits. In that unity, the infinite and the finite, spirit and matter, equal and unequal, are confounded. Hence results the absolute identity of all things; for the most general principles of the difference of things are the infinite and the finite, spirit and matter; and this distinction, which cannot constitute a real difference in the essence of the absolute unity, indicates only a diversity of modifications in the same one and universal being.

From this science of being is derived a subordinate science, the science of the universe. The world is nothing but the unity manifesting itself under the conditions of number. Taken in itself, the unity is God; considered as producing itself in number, it is the world. It there manifests itself under two principal forms. The universe being necessarily conceived as illimitable, it manifests itself therein as infinitely great; and, on the other hand, all the beings of which it is composed being themselves composites, essentially reducible to simple unities or monads, it manifests itself under this relation as infinitely small, the *minimum*. Finally, below the science of the universe ranks the science of particular or individual things, which, as such, are only pure shadows of reality.

From this it may be understood how Jordano Bruno distinguishes in the human mind three regions corresponding to these three divisions of the great whole. The *senses*, which are in relation only with particular phenomena, are like an eye which from the depth of a dark prison perceives through the cracks in the wall the colours which come from the surface of objects. The *reason* is an eye which receives through a window the light of the sun reflected by the moon; for reason regards not the light of unity in itself, but its reflection or refraction in the universe. Finally, the *intellect* resides in the highest region of the soul, as upon a height from which its glance, passing over all that is multiple, fixes directly on the sun, which is the unity of light. The senses perceive things *explicatim*, reason, *complicatim*, intellect, *summatim*.

Bruno was led by his system to maintain that good and evil, beauty and deformity, happiness and misery, have no absolute difference, but only a relative difference. According to Bayle, he has exhibited his theory as one that should free man from all fear of punishment in a future life, although, nevertheless, there are other passages in his writings in which he has adopted the idea of metempsychosis in the sense of the Hindu philosophy.

Atheism.

Atheism seems to have been maintained by Vanini, born 1596, and burned at Toulouse in 1619. His doctrine, which has nothing very remarkable, rested upon various passages drawn from the writings of Averroes, Pomponatius, and Cardan.

II. LOGICAL SYSTEMS.

THE logical works of the epoch we are surveying may be divided into two classes: the one treated solely of logic as the organ, or of the processes of reasoning; the other referred to the condition itself of human reason, that is, to the means afforded man to acquire certainty.

1. In the first relation we may notice the attempt made by Peter Ramus, born at the beginning of the sixteenth century in a village of Vermandois. He undertook the reform of logic. He reproached the logic of Aristotle, employed in the schools, as being inapplicable to the sciences, the arts, and affairs of life. In this point of view he subjected their methods to very severe criticism. But, in order to facilitate the employment of logic, he fell into an extreme the opposite of that which he blamed: for he reduced the theory of reasoning to the art of skilful disquisition. The attempt of Ramus produced great excitement in the schools; it was a progress in so far as it tended to break the classical bonds of Aristotelianism.

2. Among the logical works which made the condition of human reason their special object, we may refer to those of a school which considered the reason of man as naturally uncertain, until it attained, by means of the Christian revelation, a supernatural certainty. This class of ideas was developed by Montaigne in his apology for Raymond of Sebonde. It is perceptible in the book of the *Three Verities* by his disciple Charron. These principles were also those of the Portuguese Sanchez, professor at Toulouse, contemporary with Montaigne, from whom he probably borrowed them. Here likewise may be referred the scientific skepticism which Lamothe

Levayer maintained in the seventeenth century, in his *Discourse to show that the doubts of the skeptical philosophy have been of great use in the sciences.* Pascal in some parts of his writings, and Huet in the first part of his *Quæstiones Asnetanæ*, and in his treatise of the *Feebleness of the Human Mind,* have defended this system.

SECOND PHASE.

IMPULSE GIVEN TO PHILOSOPHY BY BACON, DESCARTES, AND LEIBNITZ.

THIS second phase may be divided into two parts. In the first we shall speak of the systems peculiar to each of these three great philosophers, as well as of the systems which are connected more or less directly with the special influence exerted by each of them.

In the second part we include the systems that have constituted the new schools, whose construction has been affected by the triple influence of the Baconian, Cartesian, and Leibnitzian philosophy together.

FIRST PART.

SECTION I.

BACON.

Historical Notices.

FRANCIS BACON, son of a celebrated English lawyer, was born at London in 1561. His superior abilities were manifested from his childhood. He was early struck with the vices of the method employed in scientific instruction. His knowledge of jurisprudence opened to him the career of public office. He played an important part in the political affairs of his country, and was made lord-chancellor, with the title of Baron Verulam, in the reign of James I. But his character was not as perfect as his genius. Bacon died in 1626. His philosophical reputation rests most of all upon two works, the one entitled *De Dignitate et Augmentis Scientiarum*, the other *Novum Organum Scientiarum*. Most of his other works relate especially to the physical sciences; some of them pertain to morals. He wrote also the commencement of a History of Great Britain, and the History of the Reigns of Henry VII. and Henry VIII.

Exposition.

Bacon laid down this principle, that the activity of the intellect is exercised only upon data primitively furnished by sensation. This principle was in many respects the soul of his philosophy; but he did not undertake to develop it in the form of a theory.

Apart from his principle, the works of Bacon in their general character may be divided into two parts: the first treats of the reform and progress of science; the second is a classification of human knowledge, with the purpose of establishing the bases of its organization.

I. *Of the Reformation and Progress of Science.*

Bacon investigates first the causes that have retarded and corrupted the sciences, then the methods which science should follow.

The causes that have retarded and vitiated science are four in number. He gives them the name of *idols*, because false science is a sort of intellectual idolatry, which pays to errors the worship due to truth.

1. Idols of the tribe, *idola tribûs*. These are prej-

udices common to all men. The human race is considered by him as a great tribe, which, in relation to the universal society of beings, has its particular principles.

2. Idols of the cave, *idola specûs*. These are individual prejudices. Every man has in his own soul a sort of dark cave, where the rays of truth become broken and lost.

3. Idols of the forum, *idola fori*. This denomination comprehends all the prejudices men reciprocally communicate to each other by the influence they exert upon each other.

4. Lastly, idols of the theatre, *idola theatri*. These are the prejudices which spring from the ascendency that philosophers and masters acquire over their disciples. Bacon gives to these prejudices the name of idols of the theatre, because he represented to himself philosophical doctors as actors, who come to play in turn their part of comedy upon the scene of the world.

Respecting the last cause of error, Bacon goes into particular developments. False philosophy has three principal branches: the rational, the empirical, and the superstitious philosophy. Rational philosophy takes up abstract notions as they present themselves, without examining them; and reason, separated from experiment, takes all the charge of constituting science. This philosophy has been very hurtful; but these evils will cease when men feel the necessity of adhering to experiment. The empirical philosophy begins with experience, but does not follow out the right road; it throws itself into hypothesis. The superstitious philosophy is an irrational mixture of philosophy and theology. Such, according to Bacon, was the philosophy of Plato and of many Christian writers, who, to conceal the weakness of their opinions, have represented them as necessarily bound up with revealed faith.

From all these causes of error comes, first, a false contemplation of nature: this was directed against Aristotle, whom Bacon accused of mutilating nature to make it fall in to the framework of his categories; secondly, a false method of demonstration, which has in all times prevailed in the domain of science. This is proved by the little harmony which has reigned among philosophers, and the barrenness of science in results applicable to the welfare of humanity. It is easy, besides, to conceive that false methods of demonstration must inevitably have predominated, if we consider the permanent causes of this general fact. The basis of experiment has been neglected. The human mind has languished in a long lethargy; for we see but three epochs, and those very brief, among particular nations, the Greeks, the Romans, and the moderns (Bacon knew nothing of Oriental philosophy), in which there was any attempt to arouse from this slumber. Men who occupy themselves with philosophy, give themselves up at the same time to a crowd of distracting pursuits: we see nowhere bodies of men united together and entirely devoted to the progress of science, and the greatest part of philosophers are led by motives of individual interest. Moreover, an excessive reverence for antiquity, which allows no change, is an obstacle to discovery. In fine, the human mind gives over, despairs of science, says everything has been done, that nothing more remains to do.

Having treated of the causes which retard and vitiate the sciences, Bacon lays down the methods which science should follow. They may be reduced to these three fundamental processes:

1. It is necessary to take facts from nature, to en-

rol the pure phenomena, without seeking at first to combine and explain them, because this premature attempt might be vitiated by preconceived notions. Such matters of observation, free from all mixture, phenomena simply as facts, Bacon calls *instantiæ naturæ.*

2. After having noted the phenomena, it is necessary, in order to aid the mind, which would be crushed under such a mass of facts, to construct tables of them, *comparationes instantiarum*, in which the phenomena should be classed in an order easy to comprehend.

3. Finally, when we have gotten these tables, it is necessary to advance to a real knowledge of nature by way of induction, either exclusive or affirmative. There are already, in all the sciences as they now exist, inductions more or less numerous. All these inductions must be referred to the *tables of instances*, and compared with the facts therein classified, in order to exclude those which do not agree with facts.

Bacon then gives the laws of induction. He constructs practical categories relating to the method of observation, as Aristotle had made logical categories for the basis of the syllogistic method. These practical categories are divided into secondary precepts, which are multiplied extremely. The following table will give an idea of the circle embraced by Bacon:

1. Prærogativæ instantiarum:
2. Adminicula inductionis:
3. Ratificatio inductionis:
4. Variatio inductionis pro natura subjecti:
5. Prærogativæ naturarum quatenus ad inquisitiones, sive quid est inquirendum prius et posterius:
6. Termini inquisitionis:
7. Reductio ad praxim:

8. Parasceue ad inquisitionem:
9. Schola ascensoria et descensoria axiomatum.

II. *Classification of Knowledge for the purpose of establishing the bases of their organization.*

This is the second part of the philosophical labours of Bacon. In the first he resembles a traveller, who, before setting out for an unknown country which he is proposing to explore, gets rid of all bad instruments of observation that may have been handed down to him, and constructs better; in the second Bacon puts himself upon the road, and, after his return from his travels, describes the places he has visited. His classification of the sciences is a cosmography of the human mind, or, in his own way of speaking, a description of the intellectual globe.

He refers all the productions of the human mind to three principal faculties: first, memory; secondly, phantasy, which, in the philosophy of Bacon, is the same as the active imagination of the schoolmen; thirdly, reason. To the memory corresponds poesy; to the reason is referred science properly speaking. History considers individual beings and facts; poesy seizes upon what the memory furnishes in order to form fictitious beings. Science, combining individual facts, generalizes and explains them. History is a guide; poesy is a dream; science is being awake.

1. History. History is divided into Natural, and Civil, or Human History.

Natural History is divided into three branches; for nature either freely follows its course, or deviates into disorder, or is subjugated by man. Natural History, therefore, comprehends the history of regular phenomena, of monstrosities, and of the arts. The first is begun, but ought to undergo a reformation; the second is not reduced to a science; the third does not exist. Bacon places it among the *desiderata* of the human mind.

Civil History, or, rather, Human History, is also divided into three branches.

First. Civil History properly so called. When incomplete, it is composed of simple memoirs ; when complete, it takes the name of chronicles if it considers events in succession, of biography if it concerns itself only with an individual, of narrative if it refers to an event.

Secondly. Sacred History allows the same classification, but there are others peculiar to it. It comprehends the history of religion, the particular history of prophecies, and the history of the temporal government of Providence.

Thirdly. Literary History, which is among the number of the *desiderata*, yet is nevertheless of the greatest importance, since it is the history of the human mind itself. Without it the mind is like Polyphemus deprived of his eye.

2. Poesy. Poesy is either narrative, that is to say, historical fiction, or dramatic, when fictitious history is represented to the eyes; or parabolic, which is a fiction designed to veil and present some truth. In the Greek mythology the fable of Pan is a cosmological parable ; that of Perseus a political parable ; that of Bacchus a moral parable.*

3. Science properly so called. As there are waters which spring from the earth, and others which descend from the skies, so there are sciences which man derives from the terrestrial world, and another

* [From the representation above, it appears that Bacon takes Poesy only in the restricted sense of Poetry as commonly understood, namely, the representation of the Beautiful in words, and thus assigns no place among the productions of the Phantasy, or creative imagination, to the other arts of the beautiful, music, painting, sculpture, and architecture.—*Ed.*]

science which comes from heaven by revelation. Revelation is the complement of all the sciences that man has created by the sweat of his brow; the *sab. bath* of the intelligence, the divine day of repose and consummation.

Human science, designated by the general name of philosophy, contains a multitude of different objects, and, therefore, as many sciences. To constitute their unity, it is necessary to have a general science, comprising a body of axioms common to all particular sciences.

The special sciences have three principal objects: God, Nature, and Man. We know nature by a ray of direct light; man by a reflex ray; God by a refracted ray.

After having said something of theology, Bacon occupies himself with natural science. It is either speculative or practical. The one penetrates into the interior of nature, the other places nature between the hammer and the anvil. The one observes, the other experiments.

Speculative science comprehends physics and metaphysics. Physics investigates the efficient causes of phenomena; metaphysics occupies itself about the abstract forms and final causes of being.

Practical science comprehends mechanics, by which name Bacon designates experimentation in general, and magic, which is experimentation applied to the production of extraordinary phenomena.

As to mathematics, Bacon regards it as a science purely instrumental. It is divided into pure mathematics, in which he comprehends only geometry and algebra, and mixed mathematics, or mathematics applied to the arts.

Science relative to man treats of human nature and of civil society.

Man being composed of a body and a soul united together, Bacon holds that, before occupying ourselves with either of these separately, it is necessary to constitute a science relating to the unity of man, which should explain everything that concerns personality and the communication between the soul and the body.

After this general science of human nature comes that which relates to the body. It is divided into as many branches as there are corporeal goods. To health corresponds medicine; to beauty, cosmical science, which comprises the arts of luxury; to strength, gymnastic science; to pleasure, music and painting.

The science of the soul treats either of its substance, to ascertain whether it is material and immortal, or of its faculties, which are either logical or moral.

Logic is either inventive or traditive; its object is either the investigation or the communication of truth. Under this second relation it comprehends grammar, rhetoric, criticism, and pedagogy.

Speculative moral science exhibits the natural history of character: practical moral science is devoted to the culture of the affections.

The second branch of the science of man refers to civil society: it is divided into three parts, because society should secure three sorts of good: 1. *Solamen contra solitudinem*; 2. *Adjuvamen in negotiis*; 3. *Adjuvamen contra injurias.*

Bacon concludes with some reflections upon theology founded upon revelation, which crowns the edifice of all human knowledge.

Observations.

1. Bacon has been a founder of methods, and not

a creator of great theories. He occupied himself with the organization of the human mind far more than with the explanation of things.

2. We shall see soon how the principle of sensualism, insinuated by Bacon, corrupted by its gradual development nearly all branches of philosophy.

3. Bacon rendered eminent service to science by putting the mind upon the track of observation, which had not been travelled by the scholastic philosophy, entangled as it was in the circle of logical processes. Yet, as a method of observation, his method is not complete: he insisted upon the observation of sensible facts, and neglected to recommend the observation of psychological facts.

4. All his efforts were directed to the object of substituting induction for the syllogistic method. Induction is really the legitimate process in the physical sciences, which, as founded upon experience, cannot admit of a superior process. In this relation the philosophy of Bacon has had useful results; but by representing induction as the sole and universal process in all branches of knowledge, he banished deduction, and consequently assumed that there did not exist in the human intelligence truths, necessary, absolute, and independent of experience except merely as the condition of their development. In this relation, that is to say, in as far as it pretended to furnish the general law of the mind, the method of Bacon was radically vicious.

5. Induction necessarily supposes the relation of effect to cause; and the whole philosophy of Bacon is based upon the principle of causality. But if there existed in the human reason nothing but elements furnished by experience, could reason ever affirm the universal principle that every phenomenon has a cause? And if it could not affirm it as an absolute

principle, would not the investigation of causes be reduced in every particular case to the creation of pure hypotheses? a result diametrically opposed to the pretensions of the philosophy of Bacon.

Continuation of the Impulse given to Philosophy by Bacon.

The principle laid down by Bacon, that sensations are the sole matter of which the tissue of human knowledge is formed, contained a whole psychology; but, before it could develop itself completely, this principle was applied to cosmology by Gassendi, to morals and politics by Hobbes. Then it produced its proper psychology in the works of Locke and Condillac; and with the aid of this development, it was applied anew to morals and politics by Helvetius, to cosmology by the Baron d'Holbach, and by the whole materialist school of the eighteenth century, of which these two philosophers are the principal types.

HOBBES.

Historical Notices.

THOMAS HOBBES, born in 1588, at Malmesbury, in England, pursued his studies at the University of Oxford. His life was disturbed by the political dissensions which rent his country, and by the hostility his own opinions awakened against him. The most celebrated of his writings is that which bears the title of the *Leviathan*, by which name Hobbes designated democracy. In his travels in France he formed relations of friendship with Gassendi and Father Mersenne, who made him acquainted with Descartes. He died in England in 1679.

Exposition.

Hobbes expressly maintained that there is no

thought which is not engendered by sensation. He joined to this principle some physiological considerations, the object of which was to explain physically the nature of sensations. He also deduced from it a very incomplete essay of psychology, in which his theory of reasoning deserves particular remark. According to him, all reasoning is reduced to seeking either the whole by the addition of all its parts, or a part by the subtraction of the rest; from whence it follows that deduction and induction are only forms of equation, which is the general process of the reason; or, in other terms, that all human cognitions should be expressible in mathematical formulas, and that everything which is not expressible in that way has no reality, or, at least, no reality accessible to our intelligence. These consequences have been drawn by modern materialists.

But it is chiefly in a moral and political point of view that the theories of Hobbes should be examined. In order to seize their connexion, it is necessary first to take notice of two fundamental consequences which he deduces from his principle concerning the origin of knowledge.

The first, relative to the intelligence, is this: all words which express the incorporeal, the infinite, have no meaning for the human mind, because they represent something not represented by sensations. They ought to be banished from philosophy as vain phantoms. He admits, however, that in virtue of the law of association, which unites the sensations, and which leads the human mind to ascend from cause to cause, we arrive at the idea of God as a physical cause, although the whole notion of the divine nature is absolutely intelligible.

The second consequence, relative to the will, is that there exists no other motive to the will than sensations of pleasure and pain, or the complex notions of happiness and misery which we form by generalizing our sensations.

In a word, sensation, or, to speak in the language of Hobbes, *sension*, as passive, is the matter of the intelligence; as active, the motive force of the will.

Now the desires, the appetites, by which each individual inclines to enjoyments, produces two general and opposite results. This desire is of right unlimited; for we cannot conceive it as limited in point of right except by subordinating it to a moral law which is not derived from sensations, and which for that reason is chimerical, at least relative to man. Every man has, then, naturally a right to everything; he has the right to acquire everything he desires; and as each individual cannot acquire everything, possess everything, except at the expense of the happiness of others, it follows that men are naturally in a state of war. See the immediate consequence of the law of enjoyment as the sole law ot man.

But, on the other hand, this state of war is destructive to security, enjoyment, and life. Consequently, the desire of enjoyment urges man to come out from this state. Now war resulting from the absolute and reciprocal independence of individuals, men cannot emerge from the primitive state of war but by renouncing their independence, and by constituting a public force whose will shall prevail over all other wills. Hence the social condition, the state, which may be established in two ways, because the sovereign force may be established in the way of institution, as when it results from a free contract, or in the way of acquisition, as when one or many individuals by violence compel other individuals to submit to their will; and, since the object to which humanity should tend, that is, the cessation of war, is attained in the second case as well as in the first, the state founded in a consent violently obtained is as legitimate as the state founded in a free convention. It results from all this that the desire of enjoyment, although unlimited in point of right in a state of nature, must be limited in point of fact in a social state in order to attain its end. See the second consequence, which is a mediate consequence of the law of enjoyment.

The theory of Hobbes supposes, then, radically a state of contradiction, of opposition, of war, not only between the individuals who compose mankind, but also between the elements of human nature itself.

Setting out with the equality of rights, founded solely upon the desire of enjoyment, Hobbes arrives at the destruction of all liberty. He lays down as a principle absolute independence, and establishes as a consequence absolute despotism; for the public force in his system is nothing but despotism conceived in its greatest strictness and extension.

In fact, the public force can be limited neither by religious law, nor by moral law, nor by civil law. It cannot be limited by religious law; religion relates to objects lying beyond the domain of human intelligence: there can, therefore, be no other reason for preferring one kind of worship to another than the public utility, which is determined by the public force, which thus rules religion, and is not ruled by it. The public force cannot be limited by moral law. In the primitive state of war, every one having a right to everything, there is neither justice nor injustice, neither right nor wrong. In the social state morality is nothing but the public utility; and here again it is to the sovereign public force it belongs to decide what is just or unjust: give this right to individuals, and the public force is destroyed. Fi nally, it cannot be limited by civil law, since civil law is nothing but an arrangement of means destined to secure the observance of the law of justice as it is arbitrarily understood and defined by the sovereign public force. Thus the public force is bound by no law whatever. It could not be limited in any degree without falling again, at least partially, into the state of war from which man emerged by society. This is also the reason why the bad administration of a state gives no right of overthrowing the governing force.

Such an overturn causes the state to retrograde to the condition of war or the destruction of society, and the worst social state is better than its destruction. Only it may happen that the public force falls to dissolution; then the social compact is likewise dissolved, and men return of necessity to independence and war in order to arrive again at a social state, that is, to a universal and absolute submission to a public force adequate to maintain the peace.

Hobbes blends with this theory maxims concerning the necessity of faithfully observing agreements and other obligations of justice and mutual benevolence. He shows very clearly that society could not exist but by the application of these maxims; but in his system, which radically abolishes the idea of rights and duties, we can find no conceivable root of any obligation whatever.

Summarily, this system is social materialism. This character is manifest even in the terms employed by Hobbes to define the notion of philosophy. Setting out with sensations, he makes the sole object of philosophy to be the study of *bodies*, which he distinguishes into two classes, *natural bodies* and *political bodies*. Physics, taken in an extended sense, becomes then the sole science, whose universal instrument is reasoning, reduced, as we have seen, to mathematical processes. In his political theories Hobbes goes into one branch of that science which modern materialists have called *social physics.*

GASSENDI.

Historical Notices.

PETER GASSENDI was born at a village of Provence in 1592. He entered the ecclesiastical state, and for some time was professor of philosophy and theology at the University of Aix. He was afterward appointed lecturer on mathematics at the Royal College of France, where his lectures attracted a numerous audience. His works against the philosophy of Aristotle and that of Descartes, as well as his *Syntagma philosophiæ Epicuri*, and his book on the *Life of Epicurus*, deserve particular attention. Gassendi's learning was very extensive and various. He was the friend or the correspondent of most of the learned men of his age. His relations with Descartes were interrupted by a philosophical quarrel, but were renewed by a reconciliation. He died in 1655.

Exposition.

Gassendi, whose mind had been nurtured by the writings of Bacon, for whom he professed the liveliest admiration, maintains, as Bacon did, that sensations are the generative source of all human knowledge. Consistently with this principle, he gave to the primitive ideas the name of simple imagination, and composed a logic in which his theory of knowledge was brought out. He reduced all intelligence to the perception of facts furnished by sensation, and to the *comparison* of facts by means of which the mind passes from singular to general notions. He had the idea of a genealogical tree, representing the growth of the human mind or the generation of ideas by sensations, as the genealogical tree of Porphyry represents the formation of logical abstractions.

Setting out from logic, Gassendi divides his philosophy into two branches, physics and morals. Like Bacon, he excludes metaphysics in the ordinary sense of the word. He did not consider speculations concerning God and the soul as derivable from a special science such as metaphysics would be: according to him, we arrive at these notions either by physics or morals.

His morals, which contains principles borrowed from the system of Epicurus, which he endeavoured to rectify in conformity with Christian views, is not the most important portion of his works. He was most of all occupied by physical theories.

Gassendi had remarked the little fruit for the progress of science which had been gathered from the abstractions of the Aristotelian philosophy applied to the study of the material world, and the obstacles opposed by this inert mass of abstractions to the true application of nature. Seeking to enlarge the path which was to lead to a more satisfactory physics, he undertook to throw out of the way these arbitrary constructions, and, in order to attack them in their basis, he made a severe criticism upon Aristotle, though rendering him justice in some respects. But to destroy is not to do everything; it behooved him also to lay the foundations of a new physical philosopy. Already Bacon had recommended the doctrine of Democritus concerning atoms as a luminous and fruitful hypothesis: already some writers, as Sebastian Basson, Beauregard, Magnen, Sennert, had attempted to revive this hypothesis. Gassendi brought forward the two principles of Epicurus, vacuum and atoms, as the primary basis of any physical theory. But he guarded his orthodoxy by recognising God as the creator and prime mover of the universe, but the creation being taken for granted, he maintained that from the atomistic doctrine the explanation of all phenomena could be deduced. His theory concerning the vacuum, which was attacked by Descartes, implied the existence of something neither spirit nor body, and which thus was excluded from the two great categories within which, according to the Cartesian philosophy, everything existing should find a place. For the rest, the physical philosophy of Gassendi had a general characteristic in common with that of Descartes; for it was the latter who said, "Give me matter and motion, and I will explain the universe." Both of them founded a mechanical philosophy, which must needs, in being developed, endeavour to refer to mathematical laws all phenomena, even the physiological phenomena which are the manifestation of life.

Among the number of the disciples of Gassendi are reckoned Michael Nuraeus in France, and Walter Charleton in England.

LOCKE.—CONDILLAC.

Historical Notices.

JOHN LOCKE was born in England, at Wrington, in the county of Bristol, in the year 1632. After having studied medicine, anatomy, and natural history, he conceived the plan of his *Essay on the Human Understanding*, upon which he meditated for twenty years, and which he published in 1690. Implicated in the political quarrels of his country, he was subjected to frequent loss of public offices and to persecutions until the revolution. He wrote an *Essay on Civil Government,* besides other writings upon religious and economical questions. In his religious belief he belonged to the Socinians. He died in 1704.

ETTIENNE BONNOT DE CONDILLAC, born at Grenoble in 1715, and died at Beaugency in 1780, was preceptor to the Duke of Parma, grandson of Louis XV. His *Essay on the Origin of Human Knowledge,* his *Treatise of Sensations,* and his *Treatise of Systems,* contain the bases and principal developments of his philosophical theories. His grammar and his logic make part of a course of study which he composed for the instruction of the prince whose education had been confided to him.

Exposition.

The principle of sensualism laid down by Bacon was particularly developed by Locke, who made it the basis of his psychology. The Essay on the Human Understanding relates to two capital questions: 1. The origin of ideas as modifications of the thinking subject; 2. The principle of knowledge, that is, of the correspondence of ideas to objects.

I. Origin of ideas. Locke admitted two sources of ideas, sensation, and reflection, which is the knowledge the mind takes of its various operations. All ideas of things distinct from the thinking subject are derived from sensation; all ideas of the modes of being, or operations of the thinking subject, the ideas of *perception, thought, doubt, belief, reasoning, knowledge, will,* are derived from reflection. This latter, though different from sensation in that it does not refer to an external object, has a fundamental characteristic in common with sensation; for both of them imply a feeling, a sentiment, and we may give to reflection the name of internal sense as a denomination which expresses at once its analogy with sensation and its difference.

Ideas, in relation to things, may in turn be divided into two classes: simple ideas, direct products of sensation and reflection, and complex ideas, which the understanding forms from simple ideas by combining these primitive elements.

Locke passes in review the principal ideas which have been or may be considered as simple and elementary.

The idea of space is given us by sight and touch; it is resolved at bottom into that of body.

The idea of time comes from the reflection of the soul on the series of ideas which follow after each other.

The idea of infinity, very obscure and purely negative, is resolved into the idea of number conceived as indefinitely repeated by the mind.

The idea of personal identity from the union of memory and consciousness, a union in virtue of which we judge that such or such a past action was done by the same being who actually represents it himself.

The idea of substance cannot be a simple idea; it is nothing but the collection or combination of simple ideas which we refer to a supposed subject. For the rest we have no clear idea of what is called substance.

The ideas of cause and effect are derived both from sensation and from reflection: from sensation, inasmuch as they express a succession of phenomena, of which one constantly takes place after the other; from reflection, because the idea of power is principally furnished by the consciousness of our own internal activity or our will.

The idea of right and wrong is radically nothing

but the idea of happiness or misery attached to the observance or infraction of a maxim proposed as a law, that is to say, to the idea of reward or punishment.

After having treated the origin of simple ideas, Locke investigates the origin of complex ideas. He undertakes to explain how, by combining simple ideas, then by combining the results of those first combinations, and so on to the end, the human mind, out of some primitive elements, by means of the law of association of perceptions, forms all the other ideas of which it is possessed.

II. Locke passes then to the question concerning the principle of *knowledge*, or the correspondence of ideas to things. As language exerts a great influence in the formation of abstract ideas, and becomes the occasion of very many errors, he first treats of the relation of words to ideas, in order to discover the illusions of which words are the source, and comes then to the relation of ideas to things, or to knowledge.

All knowledge depends upon the conformity of ideas to their objects. To prove this conformity, it would be necessary to confront the idea with its object; but, on the other hand, we know the object only by the idea itself. Locke did not solve this difficulty; he merely took for granted that all simple ideas are necessarily a representation of things.

Sensible ideas are the representation of the qualities of bodies, as ideas produced by reflection are the representation of the operations of the understanding. But, even if this were the fact, we could know on the system of Locke only the qualities of things, and never any substantial existence. To explain how sensations are representative, Locke reproduces, under a different phraseology, the old hypothesis of images or sensible species, which, coming from bodies, enter the human organism, and are transmitted by the organs to the soul.

He inquires how our ideas can be representatives of finite spirits; and as he cannot find in the ideas, as he has conceived them, the principle of such a representation, he concludes we can no more know by our ideas the existence of finite spirits than we can know the existence of fairies by the ideas which we form of them.

He has recourse to a supernatural order of instruction in order to obtain certainty as to the existence of spirits. In the system of Malebranche, which we shall presently analyze, the existence of bodies cannot be proved by the idea of spirit and that of the infinite. Now in the theory of Locke, the idea of the infinite is nothing but that of indefinite number, and no idea is representative of spirit as spirit. Consequently, there are no means of arriving logically at the idea of God, notwithstanding the efforts he has made to avoid this consequence.

The theory of Locke was developed in France by Condillac. These developments are of two sorts.

His analysis of the operations of the understanding, as well as his analysis of language, contain a multitude of considerations and observations in detail, which are modifications or complements more or less ingenious of the views of the English philosopher. But they contain nothing fundamental for the development of sensualism.

This is not the case with respect to the principle of Condillac, according to which all ideas are nothing but sensations transformed. Locke had admitted two sources of ideas, sensation, and reflection, or the consciousness which the soul has of its own operations. Condillac maintained, in the first place, that all operations of the soul are reducible to a single one, namely, attention, which exists in various degrees and under various relations, and that reflection is itself only a mode of attention. But what is attention? According to Condillac, it is nothing but the effect of a predominant sensation. Everything, therefore, becomes resolved into a single element, sensation. Thereby the unity of sensualism is constituted. Instead of two sources of ideas, there is but one: instead of two states of the soul, passive in sensation, active in reflection, the soul has but one only mode of being; it is throughout passive. This doctrine of Condillac had a more important influence in the development of sensualism than all other parts of his philosophy taken together. By this doctrine sensualism attained, in point of ideology, its utmost limit.

For the rest, the method followed by Condillac did not correspond with the principles of his philosophy. He pretended, on the one hand, to derive everything from observation, and, on the other hand, he proceeded by hypothesis; endeavouring, by the hypothesis of a statue endowed with the faculty of feeling, to explain the origin of knowledge; and by the hypothesis of two children abandoned in a desert, to explain the origin of language.

Observations.

The radical vice of the theories of Locke and Condillac is in not conceiving that there are in the human mind necessary, universal, and absolute ideas, of which sensation cannot contain the principle. This has been shown by Reid, Stewart, and many others, and especially, with great force, by Cousin in his review of the system of Locke.

These theories contain also a radical vice of method. They suppose man exercising first one of his faculties, then another, and another. But this is only a factitious man, not real man. The intellectual life implies the simultaneous working of several faculties, very much as the organic life is conditioned by the simultaneous working of many organs. There is in both an intimate inward unity, which cannot be constructed piecemeal.

HELVETIUS.

CONDILLAC applied sensualism to ideology. Helvetius (born at Paris in 1715, died in 1771), made application of it to morals. His whole theory may be reduced to this enthymeme: there is in the sphere of the intelligence nothing but sensations; there can therefore be in the sphere of the will nothing but pleasure or pain. The antecedent of this enthymeme was furnished by the dominant ideology. To prove the consequent, he rested upon the incontestable principle that the will can act only upon elements furnished by the intelligence. Now sensations, in their relation to the will, are nothing more than pleasure or pain.

The system of Helvetius contains two orders of ideas. In as far as the object is to conclude from the principles of sensualism to the morality of self-interest, as being the only possible morality, Helvetius reasons very strictly: as a matter of deduction, this part of his writings is logically unassailable. But when he endeavours to find in this moral conception the root of duties and of virtue, all the art of sophisms is unable to conceal the enormous vice of his theory. The notion of virtue implies the subordination of particular inclinations to a rule which cannot be found in the mere sphere of enjoyment, since the desire of enjoyment, taken by itself, aspires to exclude everything that would limit the gratification of particular inclinations.

Doctrines analogous to those of Helvetius were maintained by St. Lambert, and by many other moralists of the eighteenth century.

D'HOLBACH.

THIS materialist, born in the Palatinate in 1723, died at Paris in 1789. He applied sensualism to a theory of the universe, which he developed in his book entitled the *System of Nature.*

Thought is but the faculty of feeling, and sensations correspond to nothing but sensible things. All idea of spiritual beings is therefore destitute of any basis.

The senses discover to us nothing in the universe but matter endowed with certain properties and motion, which is essential to it, since matter is the only existence.

All particular beings are nothing but the different combinations which motion produces in matter.

The moving force is developed in various degrees: besides the combination designated by the term rude bodies, it produces also another combination which constitutes organized beings, and, developing itself still farther, produces effective sensibility, which is only the effect of a certain kind of organization.

All human actions are the necessary result either of the internal motion of the organization, or of external motions by which they are modified.

From his cosmological theory D'Holbach deduces consequences with respect to society fundamentally analogous to the system of Helvetius.

HUME.

WHILE sensualism was producing in France a selfish morality and an atheistic cosmology, David Hume (born at Edinburgh in 1711, died in 1776) carried it to its last consequences, and ended in skepticism.

All the modifications of the mind which are distinguished from sensations, and usually termed ideas, judgments, etc., are, according to Hume, nothing but sensations weakened by time or absence of the object, and, consequently, less certain than sensations strictly so called. But even the latter are themselves necessarily uncertain, because we have no rational basis which authorizes us to affirm that they correspond to their objects.

Although Hume attacked the certainty of all fundamental notions, his skeptical argumentation may nevertheless be referred to three principal heads.

All judgments relative to the physical world rest upon the notion of cause: all our judgments relative to the moral world imply the notion of virtue and of free-will: and, finally, every theory which would embrace at once the physical and the moral world in order to explain their origin and to conceive their unity, implies the notion of a universal principle of all being, or God.

Hume undertook, setting out with sensualism, to prove that these three fundamental notions, considered as objective cognitions, are nothing but hypotheses or factitious ideas, destitute of any foundation in the human mind.

In the physical world, experience shows us the relations of succession or simultaneousness in facts, but it shows us nothing more. Now, from the fact that A coexists with B, we cannot conclude that one depends upon the other; so, if B comes after A, we cannot any more conclude that A is the cause of B. In a word, any affirmation of cause and effect goes beyond the simple relations established by sensation, which is the sole element of human knowledge; it is the unreasonable pretension of extracting from that primitive stock of the intelligence notions of which it does not contain the germes. But, at the same time, if we renounce the idea of cause, all our judgments respecting the physical world necessarily fall to pieces. For, in the first place, we cannot begin in the slightest degree to explain the phenomena of nature except by applying the idea of cause; and, in the next place, it is by this idea, and by this idea alone, that we can believe in the existence even of bodies; we believe in them, in fact, only because we consider them as causes of our sensations.

The notions upon which rest our judgments relative to the moral world have not a more real basis. Limited necessarily within the sphere of sensations, man can have no other reasonable motive of action than the notion of his own personal interest; the idea of virtue, on the contrary, implies something distinct from selfishness; it has, therefore, no principle in the intelligence. Virtue can proceed only from a sentiment destitute of all rational motive, and which Hume compares to taste; but as this sentiment, according to his system, has no foundation which the reason can conceive, we come again on this point to skepticism. And as to the idea of free-will, we feel very clearly that we will, but we feel nothing farther. Internal experience, which establishes the fact of volition, can teach us nothing in regard to the origin of the fact which is attributed to a free power. The notion of freedom is, besides, contradictory; the free choice is not possible without motives, and every determining motive is in the last analysis only a stronger sensation, which necessarily constrains the will.

Finally, the human mind is unable to ascend by any legitimate exercise of its faculties to the notion of a universal principle of beings. If we take ground upon the elements furnished by sensation (and this is all the ground we have to go upon), we can arrive at the idea of God only by way of induction, that is to say, by considering God as the cause and the universe as the effect. The notion of cause is radically uncertain; and, even if it had any real validity within the sphere of facts of observation, it would not follow that it must have the same validity when transferred out of the sphere of human experience.

Hume applied the sensual philosophy to the history of religious beliefs. Men originally adored only the phenomena of nature, whose power appeared to them terrible or beneficent. From abstraction to abstraction, they have been transformed into gods; the human mind has formed beyond the visible world another world of its own invention.

SECTION II.

DESCARTES.

Historical Notices.

RÉNÉ DESCARTES was born at La Haye, in Touraine, in 1596. He embraced the military profession; but the life of the camp disturbed his meditations. After travelling in several countries of Europe, he retired to Holland to give himself up exclusively to the works he had planned. His great discoveries in the mathematical and physical sciences had already revealed his genius, when he published his two principal philosophical works, his *Discourse on the Method of rightly conducting reason and inves-*

gating truth in the sciences, and his *Meditations on First Philosophy*. The partisans of the philosophy of Aristotle, whom Descartes had vigorously attacked, did not always limit themselves to the use of the weapons of discussion against him. Vöet, professor of theology in the Protestant University of Utrecht, pursued him with atrocious calumnies. Christina, queen of Sweden, offered him an asylum at Stockholm, where he ended his days in 1650. At the request of the ambassador of France, his mortal remains were transported to Paris.

Exposition.

Descartes considered human science, and particularly philosophy, as an effort of human reason to deduce from first causes rules for the conduct of life and for the practical arts. Comparing the existing science of his times with this ideal standard, he concluded it was far from being conformed to it. On one hand, there were principles grounded not in reason, but in a blind confidence in the scientific traditions of the past; on the other, consequences which often had no practical results; in a word, uncertainty in its bases, barrenness in effects: such appeared to him the fundamental vices of contemporary science.

He hence concluded the necessity of reconstructing the edifice of human knowledge. He could not proceed in this reconstruction except upon the ideas of others, or upon his own. To accept, by faith in another, the principles necessary to this great work, would be to throw science into the very condition from which he wished to rescue it. It was necessary, therefore, first of all to isolate himself from all ideas received among men, and to retire into his own thoughts. But these might themselves also be an assemblage of errors, or, at least, a mixture of error and truth. There would be no means of discriminating so long as he retained a single one of those ideas as true, or conformed to reality; for the error might be found in that very idea. It was requisite, therefore, in the second place, to isolate himself from all his own ideas, that is, to hold them for doubtful, as he had already held for doubtful the opinions of others. There remained, accordingly, nothing but doubt, and he was forced to seek in it the principle of the reconstruction of all human ideas. "It is not to-day for the first time that I have perceived in myself that from my earliest years I have received a great many false opinions as true, and that what I have built upon principles so badly ascertained can be only very doubtful and uncertain. And, accordingly, I have decidedly judged that I must seriously undertake some time in my life to rid myself of all the opinions I had before taken upon trust, and begin altogether anew from the foundation, if I would establish anything firm and constant in science."

But doubt implies actual thinking, and actual thinking implies existence. I doubt, then I think; I think, then I exist: thus man finds himself in the very act of doubting. Here Descartes seized, or thought he seized, in self-consciousness, a fact and a principle. The fact was the doubting, the thinking, the existing: the principle was the relation of doubt to thought, of thought to existence. He affirmed thought as contained in the idea of doubting; he affirmed existence as contained in the idea of thinking; the perception of these relations transformed itself into this general principle: everything which is clearly contained in the idea of a thing, may be affirmed of that thing.

But hitherto Descartes had not advanced beyond

his own inward consciousness, and here the question was whether he could do so; whether, instead of possessing solely the knowledge of himself as a thinking being, he could attain, by means of thought, to a knowledge of realities external to himself. The problem to be solved was this: To find an idea which could not subsist as a conception of the mind without its object itself having also existence: an idea which could be subjectively possible only as far as it was objectively real. Descartes propounded the idea of a supremely perfect being as the principle of the connexion of the ideal and real. The idea of supreme perfection implies existence, since existence is itself a perfection. "If we ask, not in regard to a body, but in regard to anything, whatever it may be, which has in itself all the perfections which can be together, whether existence is to be reckoned among them, we may at first, it is true, be in doubt about it, because our mind, which is finite, not being accustomed to consider them except separately, may not perhaps perceive at the first glance how necessarily they are joined together. But if we carefully examine whether existence belongs to a being supremely powerful, and what sort of existence, we shall find ourselves able clearly and distinctly to know, first, that at least possible existence agrees with him, as well as with all other things of which we have in ourselves any distinct idea, even those which are composed of fictions of our own mind: and next, because we cannot think that his existence is possible, without knowing at the same time—keeping in mind his infinite power—that he can exist by his own force, we conclude that he really exists, and that he has been from all eternity; for it is very evident from the light of nature that that which exists by its own force exists always; and thus we shall know that necessary existence is contained in the idea of a supremely powerful being, not by a fiction of the understanding, but because it belongs to the true and immutable nature of such a being to exist; and it will be easy for us to know that it is impossible for this supremely powerful being not to have in himself all other perfections that are contained in the idea of God, in such sort that, of their own proper nature and without any fiction of the understanding, they are always joined together and exist in God." Thus, just as I affirm my own existence, because its idea is contained in the notion of thinking, so I affirm the existence of the supremely perfect being, because the idea of existence is contained in the very idea of such a being. The existence of an external reality rests, therefore, upon the same logical basis as the internal reality.

In his third *Meditation*, which is the one where he seeks to pass out from the consciousness of *self* to God, Descartes endeavoured to demonstrate the existence of God, not from the internal characteristics of the idea of the infinite, but from its external relations, that is to say, by ascending from the idea to the cause of the idea. He had said: My intelligence, being finite, has not derived from itself the idea of the infinite; every finite cause, of whatever sort, is equally incapable of producing it; it must have been produced in me by the infinite himself. But in his Reply to the Objections brought against him, he insisted upon the proof deduced from the internal characteristics of the idea of God. The first of these proofs, the proof *à posteriori*, supposes, besides the idea of the infinitely perfect being, the certainty of the notion of cause; the proof *à priori* supposes nothing more than the logical notion of the infinite. This proof was conceived by Descartes as only the simple affirmation of what is contained in that idea, just as the principle, *I think, therefore I exist*, was only the affirmation of what is contained in the idea of thinking. The second act of the intelligence was thus identical with the first; it was only a transformation of it. The proof *à priori* agreed, therefore, much better than the other with his fundamental process of the reason; and, accordingly, it has prevailed in the Cartesian philosophy.

We have seen what, according to Descartes, is the necessary development of the mind contemplating itself: this development is not complete except as it implies God. Without the notion of God, man might suppose that even in his clearest ideas he is the sport of an evil genius devoted to deceiving him, or, at least, he could not find in his mind anything necessarily repugnant to such a supposition. But thought, resolving itself in the last analysis into the idea of the supremely perfect and supremely true being, excludes the possibility of such an external illusion, just as primitively the idea of thinking, resolving itself into that of existence, excludes purely internal doubt.

Descartes had thus arrived at the knowledge of an external reality, the source of all reality, by applying this principle: Everything which is contained in the idea of a thing must be affirmed of the thing itself. It was by carrying out the application of the same principle that he arrived at the knowledge of all realities. But, as he was liable to make false applications of it, it was needful to inquire how man is led into error, in order to avoid error in its cause. From whence, then, comes error? Does it come from the intelligence or from the will? The intelligence produces ideas, and no idea can be false, because then the idea of a thing would not contain what it contained. Error has not, then, its root in the intelligence; it can have place only when man, by an act of will, affirms what is not contained in ideas. "From whence, then, spring my errors? from this alone, that the will being more ample and extensive than the understanding, I do not restrain it within the same limits, but I extend it also to things I do not understand, in respect to which, being in itself indifferent, it gets very easily astray, and chooses the false for the true, the bad for the good; and thus I am led to err and to sin." The general rule of human judgments is reduced, therefore, to keeping the will within the limits of the understanding.

Descartes believed he had ascertained by this series of processes, which he called methodical doubt, the foundations of human certainty. This basis being established, he began to work at the construction of the system of human knowledge.

Man finds in his consciousness two sorts of ideas: the idea of thought, and the idea of extension. All human ideas belong to these two categories; for all other ideas, whether relative to what is called soul or to what is called body, express, the first only particular attributes of thought, and the second only particular attributes of extension. And as these primary ideas are essentially distinct, he concluded that the substances whose fundamental attributes are respectively thought and extension are themselves necessarily distinct. The world, then, comprehends two classes of beings of different nature, spirits, and matter or bodies. Thus reasoning, Descartes was led to maintain that the essence of spirit is in thought, and the essence of matter in extension; and this was one of the fundamental principles of all his theories, which thus fell into two divisions, the philosophy of spirits, and the philosophy of bodies.

The theory of spirits comprehends that of God, and of man so far as he is a thinking being. The idea of God, implying unity, excludes divisibility and extension. God is then a spirit, and not a body. Sensation supposes a body: there is, therefore, no sensation in God; he is pure intelligence and pure will.

In regard to created spirits, the most remarkable part of Cartesianism is its theory of innate ideas. The intelligence possesses the idea of the infinite; and as it is at the same time a finite intelligence, it could not acquire this idea by its own operations, limited like itself. This idea, then, and all others which are a derivation, a particularization of it, are not acquired ideas: they are communicated to the mind by the Creator; they are innate. Here Descartes took the opposite extreme from Bacon, who regarded the human soul as a *tabula rasa*, a blank surface. Descartes did not, however, pretend that these ideas were innate in the sense that they were constantly present to the mind. "When I say that any idea is born with us, or that it is naturally imprinted on our souls, I do not mean that it is always present in thought, for this would be contrary to fact; but only that we have in ourselves the faculty of reproducing it."

Descartes maintained a great difference between the mode of proving the existence of spirit and that of proving the existence of body. It is true that in his system the divine veracity was the primitive and general guarantee of human ideas in the sense remarked above. But, this guarantee being supposed, we come to the conclusion that spirits exist by developing what is contained in the very notion of thought, while, by developing the notion of extension alone, we could not conclude the existence of bodies.

Thought implies in itself the existence of the thinking subject. But the notion of extension does not imply necessarily the existence of an extended object: it may be a simple modification of the mind. To demonstrate the existence of bodies requires the intervention of an element distinct from the idea; we must rest upon the natural impulse which leads us to believe in our sensations; this impulse or instinct cannot itself be conceived as having the truth for its end, except as an impulse from the author of our nature. The certainty of the existence of bodies depends, therefore, upon the divine veracity, inasmuch as it is the guarantee not only of our ideas, but of our instincts, which amounts to saying that we only *believe* the existence of bodies, while we *conceive* the existence of spirits.

Having in this way established the existence of the corporeal world, Descartes made it the second object of his speculations. Here is manifested a correlation between his theory of spirits and his theory of bodies. In the spiritual substance we distinguish thought, which is essential; then will, which is in some sort thought in motion. In the corporeal substance we distinguish extension, which is essential, and then motion produced in it. Physical philosophy is, then, radically the theory both of the immutable properties of extension and of the changeable properties which depend upon motion. All explanations, therefore, of material phenomena ought to be deduced from mechanics, resting on the basis of geometry.

Descartes applied his mechanical philosophy first to the phenomena of the inorganic world. In his metaphysics he had recognised God as the creator of matter and the prime mover of the universe. God, according to the remark of Pascal, appeared at the head of the Cartesian cosmology only to give a jerk to the world at the beginning, and to set things ago-ing. But, this done, mechanics was to explain all the operations of nature. Thus Descartes banished from physical theories all inquiries after final causes. These inquiries, according to him, were presumption, and a hinderance to the progress of science: presumption, because the limited mind of man should not pretend to discover the ends proposed by infinite intelligence; an obstacle to the progress of science, because they diverted science from the observation of efficient causes to plunge it in speculations concerning occult causes.

Descartes banished also the idea of space, in as far as different from the idea of body. The idea of space is nothing but a modification of the idea of extension; and, as extension is the essence of bodies, there can exist no space where body is wanting; in other words, a vacuum is impossible. He rejected also indivisible elements, called atoms; such an indivisibility is incompatible with the notion of extension, and extension cannot be composed except of elements analogous to it. He held, consequently, the infinite divisibility of matter, and, at the same time, its unlimited extension. To suppose the material universe actually limited, would be to suppose beyond those limits an infinite void, a thing contradictory to the principles of his philosophy.

He deduced from his ideas concerning extension and vacuum, combined with the general principles of mechanics, his celebrated theory of *vortexes*, which belongs to the history of physics. It has given way to the theory of Newton concerning gravitation. The vacuum, banished by Descartes, has reappeared in the system of his rival.

Pursuing the development of his mechanical theory, Descartes applied it to organic beings. Animals are nothing but automata destitute of any faculty of feeling. The movements which they perform, however orderly they may be, do not prove, any more than the motions of a chronometer, the existence of a thinking principle in them; and as there is nothing useless in nature, it would be unreasonable to suppose souls created merely to produce an order of phenomena which might exist without their intervention. All the phenomena of organic life manifested in brutes, and still more those manifested in vegetables, may and should be referred to the laws of motion. It is the same with the organic life of man: the sensations and passions, without doubt, have their seat in the spiritual principle, but their physical causes fall under the general theory of mechanics applied to the human organization.

If we cast a glance over the whole doctrine of Descartes, we see that his philosophy relative to the corporeal world is entirely separated from his philosophy of spirits. He had placed at the origin of all his theories two ideas, which were to contain all others, the idea of thought and the idea of extension. As there existed in his system no connexion, perceived by the mind, between these two radical ideas, the result was necessarily two orders of parallel speculations, which could never find any point of concurrence. How, then, was the action of the body upon the soul, and of the soul upon the body, or, at least, their mutual correlation, to be conceived? In this point the philosophy of Descartes had a great defect; many of his disciples, particularly Malebranche, endeavoured to fill up the chasm by the hypothesis of occasional causes, of which we shall presently speak.

Observations.

1. In regard to the philosophy of Descartes, we ought to distinguish between the theories he put forth and the impulse he gave to the human mind. Many of his theories have been abandoned; but the impulse communicated by Descartes in his resistance to the yoke of routine and the prejudices of the schoolmen has always lasted.

2. The methodical doubt of Descartes has given rise in these later times to long discussions concerning the basis and rule of human reason, to which we shall return.

3. Most philosophers have sought for a certain logical process by which to pass from the internal to the external, from thought to outward realities. Descartes resolved this question by the process adopted by St. Anselm at the earliest period of scientific organization in the Middle Ages. The solidity of the Cartesian theories depends fundamentally upon the question what validity is to be attributed to the demonstration of the existence of the infinite from the idea of the infinite.

4. In maintaining that thought is all the essence of spirit, and that extension is all the essence of matter, Cartesianism laid down the principle of a radical divorce between the spiritual and physical sciences.

5. By its theory of innate ideas Cartesianism was a reaction against the sensualism of the English philosophy of Bacon, and particularly against the nominal philosophy of Hobbes. It has also furnished powerful considerations in favour of the immortality of the soul.

6. The pretension of reducing all the physical sciences to mechanical laws has not been favoured by

subsequent developments of those very sciences. The progress of physiology, both animal and vegetable, has established that the phenomena of organic life adhere primitively to very different laws.

7. Considered in respect to its principles and its starting point, the philosophy of Descartes excited the observation of internal facts, as the philosophy of Bacon excited the observation of external facts. The latter was the flowing outward of thought towards sensations, the former was the flowing back of thought upon itself. Modern psychology was born of Cartesianism.

MALEBRANCHE.

Historical Notices.

NICHOLAS MALEBRANCHE, born at Paris in 1638, entered the congregation of the Oratory. The reading of Descartes's *Treatise on Man* determined his philosophical vocation, which he embraced with enthusiasm. He published successively his *Search after Truth; Christian Conversations; Christian and Metaphysical Meditations;* a *Treatise of Morals; Dialogues on Metaphysics and Religion;* which drew the attention of the most distinguished men of Europe. He had controversies to maintain with Arnaud, Bossuet, Father Lamy, and Regis. His labours ended only with his life. The contemplative genius of Malebranche led him to seek for peaceful seclusion. This Christian Plato loved to meditate under the shade of the beautiful trees of the college of Juilly, where his memory is still fresh.

Exposition.

The whole structure of Malebranche's philosophy rests upon the distinction between ideas and sentiments. The philosophers who had most insisted on the dualism of the human mind had confined themselves for the most part to opposing sensations to ideas. Malebranche dug deeper into this dualism; he remarked that the element opposed to ideas, or, at least, essentially distinct from them, had a characteristic peculiar to itself, independently of the various causes which might produce it; that this element consists in the sentiment which informs the soul of its modifications, whatever might be the origin, internal or external, of the sentiment itself.

Ideas are the sight, the vision of the mind. Now non-being, having no properties, is not visible. To see nothing and not to see anything are the same thing. Ideas are, then, only the vision of something which exists; an idea is, therefore, not a simple modification of the soul, but the manifestation of an object really existing out of the soul.

It is not so with the sentiments. Thereby the mind conceives nothing; it is only made aware of its actual state, without explaining, without comprehending it; sentiment is nothing but a confused echo of a simple modification of the soul.

The subjects of ideas are eternal, immutable, necessary; either they do not appear to the mind, or they appear in that character. Sentiment corresponds only to modifications which might or might not be.

It follows from these principles that everything of which we have an idea exists, and it is in vain to object that we have frequently an idea of things which do not exist. This objection rests upon a confusion of ideas with sentiments; and, in order to make it clear, let us take two examples, one in the moral world, the other in the purely physical world.

In the first place, I imagine a man performing a

good and just action. If that man really existed, I could not be made aware of his existence and of his action but by my sensations, or, in the last analysis, by simple modifications of my own soul. In representing to myself that action which does not actually exist, I remain, therefore, in the domain of sentiment, I do not enter into that of ideas. The object, the sole object of the idea, is not the action, but the good quality of the action; and this quality is nothing but a particularization of what the mind conceives as an eternal reality, namely, justice or rectitude. By the idea I see what is; in the way of sentiment my soul is modified without any object of that modification existing.

Consider next the notions which we form of what is called the world of bodies. Everything which the mind therein conceives is reduced to relations of figure, and all relations of figure are resolvable into the general idea of extension, which particularizes itself in such or such a figure. This intelligible extension is very different from actual extension. The latter is determinate, limited; the former is conceived as infinite, since it contains all possible figures; but, although purely intellectual, it is supremely real, since it is infinite, and all the relations of figures which subsist in it are immutable and necessary. But if we have the idea of intelligible extension, we have only the sentiment of actual and determinate extension. Sounds, colours, in a word, everything that does not fall within the relations of figures, make nothing conceived by the mind, but only apprize it that it experiences such or such a sensation by occasion of a body which it believes to exist. This being established, when we represent to ourselves an object which does not really exist, what do we see? Our mind sees the figure which we attribute to it, and its relations with other figures ; now all this exists really in the intelligible extension. As to the colours and other analogous properties which we give it in imagination, they express not the objects of ideas, but the objects of our sentiments ; and, although the object of our sentiments does not exist, the object of our ideas subsists none the less. Everything which is relative to *sentiment* may or may not be ; but here, as before, we can *conceive* of nothing which has not existence.

Setting out with this theory, we must conclude that philosophy rests only on the connexion of ideas. Wherever this connexion is broken, wherever ideas fail and give way to sentiment, the mind remains in darkness. The philosopher should therefore seek for an idea to which he can attach by indissoluble bonds the whole chain of human ideas.

After the example of Descartes, Malebranche places the principle of science in the idea of God, or of the infinitely perfect Being. On the one hand, this idea implies the existence of its object ; and, on the other, the idea of the infinite contains all other ideas, which can never be anything but particular aspects of the one universal idea of being. And as the idea of self, of the me, which is the starting-point of philosophy, is finite, it follows that the finite coexists with the infinite. From hence the idea of creation, since the notion of the finite does not imply that of necessary existence.

The universe is the most perfect which could exist. God, contemplating all possible worlds, could not have wished to realize a less perfect world in preference to a world in which the divine perfections would be more completely reflected. For there could be no reason for preferring the less to the more perfect, and choice without reason would be contrary to the divine wisdom. But it should be remarked that the perfection of the world supposes that God, who is the sovereign power and the sovereign wisdom, acts by laws the most general and simple, just as finite agents act according to laws as much less simple and as much less general as they themselves are less wise and powerful. Placing ourselves in this point of view, we conceive how that which we take for imperfection in the work of the Creator is inherent in the very perfection of his work. These apparent imperfections are a sequence of the most general, that is, the most perfect laws; and the world is better with its general laws, spite of their particular inconveniences, than it would be by the suppression of the inconveniences, involving, as it would, the destruction of general laws.

But of what beings is the universe composed? Do there exist spirits and bodies? Does there exist even a difference of nature between spirits and bodies?

The idea of body or of matter resolves itself into that of actual extension. Is extension a substance or a mode? We cannot think of a circle or a square without thinking of extension; squareness and roundness are therefore only modifications of extension. But we can think of extension without thinking of anything else; it is, therefore, not a simple mode, it is a substance. Now the idea of extension does not imply that of thought: consequently, matter, whose essence is extension, must be, if it really exist, a substance essentially different from the thinking substance or spirit.

This distinction being established, it is clear that God, in creating the world, was behooved to give birth to a world of spirits. For he produces that which is most perfect; and beings capable of thinking, that is, of knowing and loving, are evidently of a nature superior to that of body. Thus the existence of spirits is contained in the very idea of creation.

But does the connexion of ideas lead us equally to acknowledge the existence of bodies? In the first place, we conceive no necessary connexion between the impressions which are called sensations and the existence of external objects, since God, by the efficacy of his infinite power, might produce these same impressions if the corporeal world did not exist. If these impressions, considered in themselves, do not prove its existence, we must go higher; we must, as Descartes has done, combine the natural instinct which leads us to believe in the testimony of our senses with the veracity of God. But here again the chain of ideas is broken, when we wish to make it result in the existence of bodies. Without doubt, the veracity of God would be an infallible guarantee of our sensations, if the instinct which leads us to refer our sensations to external objects was really invincible. But it is not: God furnishes us with a means of resisting this impulse, and this means is the possibility conceived by us of sensations as constant and as uniform without the intervention of bodies as with their intervention. Malebranche concludes, therefore, that the existence of bodies cannot be known with certainty except by revelation.

The objection has been made to this last opinion that it is reasoning in a circle, since revelation itself supposes faith in the senses which attest the facts implied in the idea of revelation. But the partisans of the philosophy of Malebranche contend that it avoids this paralogism. Even if bodies do not exist, still we must always admit that the sensible impressions respecting revelation are produced in us by divine power. Now it would be repugnant to the wisdom of God to produce such a system of appearances, if these appearances did not actually contain a divine revelation. This laid down, it would, they say, be indeed a vicious circle to conclude the existence of bodies from revelation, and revelation from the existence of bodies. But this is not the case. From sensible appearances, whether the phenomena are or are not connected with real bodies, we conclude the existence of a divine revelation on the ground of the divine wisdom. Then, hearkening to the divine word, without pretending to know beforehand whether bodies have a substantial existence or not, we learn that it expressly teaches their existence. Thus we recognise, upon the authority of revelation, that our sensible impressions do correspond to external objects called bodies; and we have admitted revelation by merely combining the fact of sensible impressions with another term, to wit, the divine wisdom.

But if the universe is composed of two sorts of beings—of spirits, whose existence is demonstrated, and of bodies, whose existence is revealed—the general notion of the universe depends upon the idea we form of the relations that exist between these two parts of creation. Are they independent of each other, or do they reciprocally act upon each other? It is a fact, that when my soul wills it, a motion is produced in my arm, and by my arm in other bodies which it displaces. It is a fact, also, that sensations spring up in my soul as if they were a result of the action of the bodies that surround me. But the thinking substance and the extended substance are so essentially independent of each other, that it is impossible to admit that the one should produce a modification of the soul, which is a spiritual effect, and that the other should produce a material effect, such as motion. This reciprocal action is therefore only apparent; the correlation which exists between mind and body results from the general laws established by the Creator, according to which he himself produces both the motions of body by *occasion* of volitions of the soul, and the impressions or sensations of the soul by *occasion* of the presence of bodies. In both cases God alone is the real and immediate cause of these effects; spirits and bodies are nothing but *occasional causes.*

From the general notion of the universe he passes to the theory of mind and body, to psychology and to physics.

The general principle of physics is that all bodies are homogeneous, since extension, which is their essence, is the same in all. Material phenomena are nothing but differences in the external form of bodies, and in the configuration of the insensible particles of which they are composed, or differences in the relations of distance. All changes which take place in bodies are consequently produced by motion, which modifies both the external or internal form of the bodies, and the relations of distance which exist between them. And as matter or extension implies no idea of motion, all the motions of nature are an immediate and permanent impulse of divine power, which acts conformably to sovereign wisdom, according to laws the most simple and general. That which is called the concussion of bodies is not the real cause of the communication of motion, it is only the occasional cause.

The theory of spirits is divided into two parts: the one treats of the intelligence, the other of the will.

The intelligence, as has been said, lives and subsists only in ideas, and ideas are the divine essence. It follows from this, first, that we see everything in God, even the corporeal world. For that which we really see in material nature is the intelligible infinite, necessary extension, which is God himself; the rest is not the object of the vision of the mind. We do not really see it, we feel it; and the obscure sentiment attests only the modifications of our soul.

It follows, in the second place, that intelligence is a perpetual revelation. Ideas not being in us, but out of us, it is God who produces them in our mind. But he does not produce them except by occasion of the attention which we will to bestow upon them. Thus God is the efficient cause of ideas; the attention of man is the occasional cause.

It follows, in the third place, that progress in knowledge depends upon the strength of attention; and, as this power is limited, as well as the capacity of the soul, in order to derive from it the greatest advantage possible, we ought to withdraw it from the dark region of sentiment, and to concentrate it upon the luminous region of ideas.

It follows, lastly, that error results only from the confusion of ideas and sentiments. It is an attempt to transform a sentiment into an idea, or to degrade an idea to the condition of a sentiment.

This theory of the intelligence leads to a corresponding theory of the will. As God is at once the cause and the object of our intelligence, so he is at once the cause and object of our love. Our invincible love of good in general is nothing but an impulse of the love with which God loves his own nature or the immutable order of the universe, just as our knowledge of the true is nothing but a communication of the ideas by which he knows himself. Our particular desires are the occasional cause of the good that is done by [in] us, just as our attention is the occasional cause of the light which enlightens our soul.

But, as we can turn our attention from the contemplation of ideas, to wander and dissipate it in the shadows of sentiment, so we can pervert our desires from the immutable world represented by ideas, to fasten them in a sort upon the series of false judgments which sentiment leads us to pass. When we search for truth in our own mere modes of feeling, it is error; when we seek there for good, it is vice.

In a word, everything that there is positive and substantial in love or the emotion of the soul, is produced by God: we produce, not that love in itself, but only good or bad applications of that love.

Resuming the foregoing principles, we comprehend both the nature of man and the duties that flow from it. God is, by his power, the efficient cause of all motions executed by the body; our will is only the occasional cause. In this first relation, our fundamental duty consists in regulating our motions according to clear ideas, as God regulates his activity according to a clear view of all things. God is, by his intelligence, the efficient cause of all our ideas; our attention is only the occasional cause. In this second relation, our fundamental duty is to concentrate our attention upon ideas, and to consult them perpetually. God is, by his love, the efficient cause of ours, or of our inclination to happiness; our desires are only the occasional cause of our participation in happiness. In this relation our duty is to connect our desires with ideas, just as the Holy Spirit is united to the Word.

Malebranche endeavoured in many ways to combine his philosophical theories with Christianity.

From his doctrine of optimism he concluded that the incarnation of Christ was a necessary condition of the perfection of the creation itself. Without this intimate union of God with humanity, and through humanity with nature, the world would not have been as perfect as it could be; it would not have been worthy of God, since God cannot prefer the less perfect to the more perfect.

From his theory of ideas and sentiments he concluded that the propensity which inclines men to look rather to liveliness of sentiment than to clearness of ideas was the indication of a profound disorder in his being; a disorder which supposes an original fall, with which is connected the doctrine of redemption.

From the principle that the divine wisdom, choosing always the most perfect means, must act by laws the most simple and general, he inferred that the laws by which grace was distributed corresponded to the laws of the creation. He recognised in nature the symbols of the supernatural world.

Observations.

1. Malebranche endeavoured to imprint upon his philosophy the characteristics of simplicity and unity which God had, in his view, given to the laws of creation. All parts of his system, which is very fruitful in varied applications, refers to some general principles with which they were in his view strictly connected. The unity of his conceptions is even more remarkable than their extent.

2. His theory of ideas is in many respects a reproduction of that of Plato. But he made it his own by his profound analysis of ideas and sentiments; by showing that if ideas are the vision of the infinite being, participated by creatures, sentiments are the consciousness of their limits. By the theory of intelligible extension he wished to fill up a chasm in Platonism which did not explain how the physical universe could be the object of ideas. The system of the vision of all things in God crowned that elevated psychology.

3. The philosophy of Malebranche runs into idealism, in the same sense that it excludes from the domain of rational speculation the notion of the existence of bodies. This notion is rested neither upon a natural belief nor upon a philosophical demonstration. It results, on the other hand, from his theory of intelligible extension, that we see everything in the corporeal world except bodies. It results also from his system of occasional causes, that, properly speaking, we do not even feel bodies which are not represented as acting in any way upon the soul.

4. Malebranche has been reproached with having wished to establish that God is the only being really active; from whence it has been concluded that his philosophy contains the germes of pantheism. But it should be observed that he maintains an activity of creatures, which is to the divine activity what the substance of creatures is to the divine substance. Finite activity supposes infinite activity, as finite existence supposes the finite.

5. The philosophical style of Malebranche is a model of clearness and modest elevation. A serene light is diffused over all his writings. No metaphysician has conceived things in a manner more intellectual, and none has expressed them in a manner more enlivened by sensuous imagery.

BERKELEY.

George Berkeley, bishop of Cloyne in Ireland, was born in 1684. He died in 1753. His principal writings are, *The Principles of Human Knowledge, Dialogues of Hylas and Philonous.*

The idealist doctrine of Berkeley destroys the existence of the corporeal world. We can know substances only by the qualities inherent in them. Now there exists no quality which we can conceive as inherent in a corporeal substance. There exist two species of qualities called sensible: primary qualities, reducible to extension, and secondary qualities, such as colour, odour, savour, etc. The Cartesian philosophy has demonstrated that the secondary qualities do not exist in the bodies, but in us; that they are not properties of an external object, but modifications of the internal principle of the soul. Now, according to Berkeley, we ought to pass the same judgments concerning the primary qualities or extension. He maintains that all the arguments by which it is proved that odour, colour, etc., do not reside in the bodies, apply equally to extension, the notion of which besides contains, according to him, contradictions which cannot be removed except by considering extension, not as an entity, but a simple conception. And as we know matter only by extension, Berkeley concluded that the material world is only phenomenal, and that there exists nothing but spirits. He believed that he had found in this doctrine the means of destroying in their very foundations the materialist systems to which the empirical philosophy of Locke had given rise in England, and which were already threatening the subversion of the whole moral order.

SPINOZA.

Benedict Spinoza was born at Amsterdam in 1632, and died in 1677. He had been brought up in Judaism, which he renounced to embrace opinions destructive of all religious belief. He revived material pantheism.

Many writers, and even Leibnitz himself, have pretended that Spinozism was born of Cartesianism. It has been noted that Spinoza commenced his career of metaphysical speculation by an exposition of the Cartesian philosophy; that he was at first nurtured in that philosophy; and that he afterward developed his system of pantheism with a great parade of terms and notions borrowed from the logic and ontology of Descartes. But from his use of those notions it does not follow that he deduced from them correct consequences.

It has been pretended, also, that the definition of substance given by Descartes contains necessarily the foundations of Spinozism. Descartes had said that a substance is that which needs nothing else in order to its existence: from which it seemed to result, that all finite beings, having need of God in order to exist, could be conceived only as simple attributes of the sole substance or of the divine Being, who alone exists independently of any other thing. The Cartesian philosophers have, however, explained the definition of substance in a very different sense from that which Spinoza attributed to it. They said that a substance is that which has no need of anything else as the subject in which it resides, *tanquam subjecto;* but that a substance may have need of something else as its principle and cause, *tanquam principio et causâ.* This distinction presupposed, it follows indeed that God is the only complete and absolute substance, since in no respect, under no relation, has he need of anything else; but it also follows that finite beings, although they have need of God as their principle and cause, may be substances, incomplete to be sure, but real, since they are conceived as subjects of attributes, and not as simply attributes of a subject.

It was this very distinction that Spinoza undertook to destroy by using other principles maintained by the Cartesian philosophy. He pretended that the principles which Descartes had employed to demonstrate the existence of two distinct substances, spirit and matter, led, on the contrary, to the conclusion of the absolute identity of substance, in the sense that all particular beings could be conceived only as attributes of a single subject. The Cartesian definition rested on the distinction between substance and cause; it implied that there existed, or might exist, not only substances, subjects of attributes, but a substance, the productive cause of other substances. Now, according to Spinoza, this production is contradictory. For either the substance which produces and the substance produced have different attributes, or they have the same attributes. If they have different attributes, we cannot conceive that one should be the cause of the other, since a cause cannot produce what it does not contain. If, on the contrary, they have the same attributes, they are not distinct. How, in fact, did Descartes prove that mind and matter are distinct? On this ground alone, that thought, the attribute of the one, is not extension, the attribute of the other. You cannot, then, said Spinoza, affirm the distinction of the substances, except on the ground of the distinction of their attributes; and, therefore, if the substance which you suppose creative and the substance which you suppose created have the same attributes, they cannot be two different substances.

All the arguments of which Spinoza availed himself to establish his fundamental principle are only developments, under very complicated and sometimes not very intelligible forms, of the dilemma to which we have just reduced his reasoning. Bayle has made the observation that this dilemma did not demonstrate what Spinoza desired to demonstrate. It follows from it, says Bayle, that two substances which have the same attributes are not different specifically; but it does not follow that there cannot exist with the same attributes two substances individually or numerically distinct. This observation applies to the second part of Spinoza's dilemma; and as to the first part of it, that if the cause must contain everything that is in the effect, it does not follow that it must contain it in the same manner or under the same mode; that the infinite cause may contain pre-eminently, that is, under a perfect or infinite mode, that which it communicates to the effect under a finite mode; and, accordingly, though created substances should have the same attributes as the substance which produced them, in the sense that they are found pre-eminently in the latter, they have, nevertheless, attributes essentially different, in the sense that what is imperfect in them is perfect in their cause.

After having endeavoured to establish that all the various realities can be known only as attributes of a sole substance, Spinoza inquires into the nature of that substance, whether material or spiritual. We must judge of the nature of a substance by its attributes. Now, according to the philosophy of Descartes, there exist but two fundamental attributes, extension and thought; and, by the admission of the Cartesians, extension supposes a material substance. Appropriating their arguments on this point, and rejecting the arguments by which they inferred the existence of spirit from the existence of thought, Spinoza pretended that thought, like extension, could be only a property of the material substance, existing simultaneously under these two attributes.

From this ontology Spinoza deduced a multitude of consequences, which he applied to psychology, to morals, and to politics.

In psychology he considered intelligence and will as simply modifications of the organism.

In morals he radically destroyed the notion of right and wrong, as incompatible with a system where everything is identical, where everything that happens is a necessary result of the energy of the sole substance.

In politics he maintained also, very consistently, that everything which is commonly designated by the name of rights is reduced to the notion of force. It followed, indeed, from his moral doctrine, essentially allied to his metaphysical doctrine, that justice relatively to each being can be conceived only as the measure of his power, since, in order to conceive it under any other notion, we must return to the ideas of an obligatory divine law and of free-will: two things evidently excluded by his fundamental principle.

Spinoza thus reached, as the last consequence of his principles, the same monstrous maxims to which Hobbes had arrived by an opposite route. The English philosopher set out from the diversity of human individuals as naturally hostile: the Dutch Jew started from their absolute identity. The one excluded from the social theory the notion of the infinite element, the principle of moral obligation; the other excluded the notion of finite beings, subjects of these obligations; and both constructed the politics of force, which transformed itself in the system of Hobbes into pure despotism, in the system of Spinoza into pure anarchy.

LOGIC.—CRITICAL SKEPTICISM.

Besides the theoretical results of the impulse given to philosophy by Descartes, we should also notice here two other sorts of philosophical exertion put forth in opposite directions, the Port Royal logic, and the critical skepticism of Bayle, who was born in the old county of Foy in 1647, and died in Holland in 1706.

The logic of the Port Royal is a combination of the principles of Descartes with those of Aristotle. It furnishes the art of demonstration by taking for granted, as the rule of all legitimate employment of artificial logic, the fundamental processes upon which Cartesianism made all certain knowledge of truth to depend.—The critical labours of Bayle were intended, on the contrary, to shake the certainty of human knowledge, and take away all confidence in demonstrations, by bringing forward upon the most important questions contradictory arguments. His captious dialectics respected none of the truths upon which religion and morality rest. In this skeptical point of view he did not spare the Cartesian philosophy, of which he had at first been a partisan.

[It should be added, that the speculations of Descartes and Malebranche were also combated by skepticism in an entirely different spirit from that of Bayle—a skepticism employed in the interest of revealed religion.

In France, *La Mothe le Vayer* had denied the existence of any rational principle as the basis of religious truth, and maintained the principle of faith, implanted by divine grace, as the ground of religious knowledge. His disciples, *Sorbiere* and *Foucher*, propagated skepticism in the same spirit, and opposed the philosophy of Descartes and Malebranche.

In England, *Joseph Glanvill*, who died in 1680, likewise advanced the principles of skepticism in relation to science, in order to limit the pretensions of dogmatic speculation.

Jerome Hirnhaym, doctor of theology at Prague, who died in 1679, gave also a religious tendency to skepticism. He declaimed with much talent against the vanity and ignorance of speculative philosophers. He admitted no axiom of reason that might not be nullified by revelation. The sole grounds of certain knowledge were divine revelation, supernatural grace, and inward illumination by God's spirit. In practical morality he deduced from his skepticism an extravagant asceticism.

At this period skepticism was quite generally employed, from pious intentions, by learned Romanists, in order to bring back Protestants to the Church.

SUPERNATURALISM.—MYSTICISM.

THE consequences of the empiricism of Hobbes on the one hand, and of the speculative rationalism of Descartes and Malebranche on the other, excited also a reaction in the direction of supernaturalism and of mysticism, though divine revelation, as the source of philosophical truth, was held in a less restricted sense than by the writers just mentioned.

Theophilus Gale, who died in 1677, maintained that true philosophy was contained originally in the word of God addressed to his people, and since then revealed to other nations at different epochs and in various ways.*

Ralph Cudworth, who was born in 1617 and died in 1688, adopted the same opinion, but applied it with much greater originality to the defence of religion against materialism and atheism. In his profound and learned work on the Intellectual System of the Universe, he gave demonstrations of the existence of God and of creation out of nothing. He maintained innate ideas in the sense of Plato, and derived therefrom a proof of the divine existence. Rejecting Malebranche's theory of occasional causes, in order

* Theoph. Gale, Philosophia Universalis, Lond., 1676 Aula Deorum Gentilium, Lond., 1676.

to explain the forms of things and the reciprocal influence of mind and matter, he framed the hypothesis of a *plastic nature*, a spiritual but unintelligent principle. This is nothing but Plato's soul of the world, distinct from God and an instrument of God. He adopted this hypothesis in order to oppose, on the one hand, the doctrine of blind chance in the creation and changes of the world, and the doctrine of mechanical necessity, and on the other, the notion of immediate and perpetual creation on the part of God. He censured Descartes for banishing from physics the consideration of final causes.

Against the moral system of Hobbes he wrote his Treatise concerning eternal and immutable Morality.

In this treatise he taught that our ideas of good and evil are not communicated either by sense or experience; we neither acquire them from instinct, nor by deducing from instinct the notion of our greatest good. Reason instantly conceives them, from a contemplation of human actions, as absolutely as it conceives the idea of cause from the contemplation of events, or of space from that of bodies. We do not deduce the idea of cause from that of an event perceived, though the latter is the occasion of the former; neither do we deduce the ideas of good and evil from actions perceived; actions are the occasion of awakening the ideas, which, when once conceived, become universal, being immediately apprehended by reason. These ideas come from the divine mind, which is their proper, eternal home, and of which human reason is an emanation. These ideas are latent in our minds till external occasions awaken them. Here also is the doctrine of Plato. Cudworth reproduced it in order to prove that our moral ideas have not the relative character supposed in the system of Hobbes. Actions are not good on account of their relation to our sensitive nature, and therefore transient and contingent. The idea of good is independent of every particular act and of every individual being. It is as eternal and immutable as the Deity. Our reason does not create it, but necessarily conceives it. With the idea of good is associated the idea of obligation; and this idea is equally immutable. Finally, the idea of good is simple and indefinable.

Henry More, who was born in 1614 and died in 1687, addicted himself more particularly to the doctrines of the New-Platonists. He wrote likewise an apology for the Cabala. He held intellectual intuition as the source of all philosophical knowledge, and maintained that all the true and legitimate notions which philosophy possesses proceeded from a divine revelation. He attempted to establish the existence of an immutable space, distinct from all mutable matter, as the principle of all life and all motion, both in the spiritual and material world. Reality consists in extension. God himself, in his being and absolute substance, is space. The human soul and the soul of animals are simple and yet extended. In morals, the science of living wisely and happily, he combines the principles of Plato and Aristotle.

Samuel Parker, a contemporary of Cudworth and More, who died in 1688, likewise attacked with severity the doctrines of Descartes, particularly his atomistic physics and his proof of the divine existence.

John Pordage (born about 1625, died in 1698, at London) wrote expressly in favour of mysticism, and attempted to reduce the theosophic extravagances of Jacob Bœhme to a system, pretending to have learned the truth of those ideas by a special revelation. His disciple, *Thomas Bromley,* propagated his opinions.

To these names may be added that of *Richard Cumberland* (born in 1632, died in 1718), who in a more philosophical way attempted to refute the principles of Hobbes, particularly in relation to morals. He endeavoured to establish the fundamental truths of morals independently of revelation and by the method of observation. He maintained disinterested virtue in opposition to the selfish system of Hobbes. But he did not, like Cudworth, attribute our moral ideas to reason; he made the principle of virtue to consist in a sentiment of benevolence towards God and towards man.]

SECTION III.

LEIBNITZ.

Historical Notices.

Godfrey William Leibnitz, born at Leipsic in 1648, wrote at first upon jurisprudence. He afterward formed the plan of an encyclopedia which embraced all branches of science, the mathematics, physics, history, morals, public law, metaphysics, theology. After having been attached for some years to the chancery of the Elector of Mayence, he was appointed counsellor by the Duke of Brunswick. He visited France, Holland, England, and Italy, formed friendships with the most celebrated men of science, and carried on a scientific correspondence with many of them. Leibnitz worked with indefatigable ardour: it is said to have often happened that he would not leave his chair for some weeks at a time. He died in 1716. He did not publish any work in which his philosophical views are united into a systematic body. Some Latin theses which he had printed at Leipsic present a summary of them in the form of articles; we shall follow these in our exposition of his fundamental doctrines.

Exposition.

Leibnitz rejected the sensualism propounded in principle by Bacon and developed by Locke, whose book on the Human Understanding appeared to him a very slender performance.

He maintained that sensations cannot be the source of notions which correspond to necessary truths, and that these notions are derived from an internal light, which is a participation in the infinite reason. But he did not confine himself to opposing sensualism; he threw himself into the opposite extreme. Not that he pretended that ideas alone constituted human intelligence; he admitted the distinction between sensations and ideas in the sense that sensations are the representations of facts, and ideas the representations of necessary truths. But, as we shall presently see, he was led by the general principles of his philosophy to conclude that sensations have not an external origin, but only an internal; that they are solely the result of the activity of the soul, which produces them without the concurrence of any principle out of itself. In the system of Locke, all notions have an external source, even the most abstract; in the philosophy of Leibnitz, they all, even sensations, have an internal source.

All branches of the philosophy of Leibnitz have a common trunk in his ontology or theory of substances: we must first comprehend that.

Man is immediately in connexion with the universe, of which he himself forms a part. Now the universe and the beings it contains present themselves to us as compounded. There cannot be composites without components; if these latter are themselves composites, they will also have their components, until we come in thought to components which are not composites, that is, to simple beings, or beings without parts, which may be termed monads, in order to express their unity, their indivisibility, their simplicity. The monads are the only real substances, for everything which is not a monad must be a composition of monads, and the composition is not a substance, but simply a relation.

From this first step Leibnitz separates himself from Descartes. The Cartesian philosophy admitted two different substances: matter, whose essence was extension, and spirit, whose essence was thought. From the principle laid down by Leibnitz, it followed, on the contrary, that there exists but one kind of substances, simple substances: that which is designated by the term matter can be nothing more than an aggregation of monads, and extension is nothing but the phenomenon which manifests this aggregation.

Investigating the essence of the monad, Leibnitz believed he discovered three principles:

1. An internal principle of variation: no monad that is not infinite implies immutability; as finite it is subject to change; and, in fact, the universe is subjected to a law of variation. Now changes could not take place in the aggregations of monads without a pre-existing change in the monads themselves. But the principle of these changes is necessarily internal; for the monad, for the reason that it is without parts, cannot be modified by an external principle, that is to say, by the action of another monad.

2. Here is seen, again, a radical separation between Leibnitz and Descartes. All the changes that take place in the universe, all phenomena without exception, are referred by Leibnitz to a force internal in each simple substance. Descartes, on the contrary, explained all the phenomena of the material universe by the communication of motion, that is, by a princi-

ple external to each body affected. In the view of Leibnitz every change resulted from a dynamic cause; Descartes acknowledged only a mechanical cause. Changes in things are wrought actively from within outwardly: changes are wrought passively from without inwardly: such were the two opposite formulas which disputed the theory of the universe. In this respect the cosmology of Leibnitz was to the cosmology of Descartes what its psychology was to that of Bacon.

3. Leibnitz held that in the essence of the monad there was a second principle, which produced the variety of the monads; a *schema*, which constitutes the peculiar characteristic, the intimate, essential, specific form of each of them. Not only has every monad qualities, for otherwise it would not be a being, but the qualities of each monad should have a character which determines their difference from other monads. Two radically undistinguishable from each other would be but one and the same thing under different names. Without this differential character there would not exist a plurality of monads; there would be but one. There would be, accordingly, neither composites nor components, and the notion of the universe would disappear.

This was, again, the antithesis of the physical theories of Descartes. According to the French philosopher, extension, the essence of matter, was identical in all bodies, and the difference of bodies resulted, not from anything internal to each, but from the general laws of motion, which produced various combinations in that universally the same extension.

4. Finally, the monad, as conceived by Leibnitz, should imply multiplicity in unity. Every change is wrought by degrees; something changes, something remains: therefore every simple substance, from the

very fact of its being subject to a law of change, contains in itself a plurality of susceptibilities, modifications, and relations, that is, to multiplicity in unity.

Leibnitz concluded from these considerations that every monad is representative of the universe. In virtue of its principle of internal variation, it can change or develop itself indefinitely. If it were composed of parts, the number of its possible variations would be limited proportionably to the number of its parts. But as it is absolutely simple, we cannot conceive any necessary limit to the development of its activity: it comes into no condition that may not be replaced by another. It contains in itself, therefore, the capacity of all modes of possible being, and thereby is representative of the whole universe.

This variation of the monads, which implies the representation of the universe, is nothing else than what is called perception. The basis of this capital thesis of the philosophy of Leibnitz may be conceived in the following manner. Thought exists in the monads, that is, in a certain number of them. Now what is thought? Properly speaking, it is consciousness, or distinct perception of the changes which go on within the monad. Thought supposes, therefore, anterior to itself, a confused perception of these changes; for we can no more conceive that a perception should spring from that which was in no sense a perception, than that a motion should spring from that which was no movement. Every clear perception must be the development of an obscure perception; all consciousness, properly speaking, is the apprehension or coming to the understanding of a vague, insensible consciousness.

Perception may therefore exist in two states: the state of perception simple and as yet confused, and the state of distinct perception, which may be designated by the term apperception. In lethargy, deep sleep, or swoon, the soul is not without perception, for then it would be destitute of activity; and if it once became entirely passive, it could not become active again. Nevertheless, the soul in those states does not experience any distinct sentiment. This state represents to us that of simple monads. The simple monads are, as it were, souls struck with stupor.

The state of distinct perception has itself two degrees. We may distinguish only the simple facts corresponding to what is called sensations. Such is the state of animals, and of men so far as animals. To this knowledge may be joined the knowledge of the truths of reason, or necessary truths. Thus is the state peculiar to man.

The general law of perception is a law of union; for, on the one hand, a perception can spring only from a perception. As any actual change in a monad is in sequel to an anterior change, so is it the germe of a future change. On the other hand, the monad being representative of variety in unity, this representation, at once one and multiple, implies an intimate connexion of perceptions.

Thus the connexion of confused perceptions with distinct perceptions, even though we may be unconscious of it, is none the less real. When we come out from the state of stupor, so to say, the primary perceptions of which we become conscious are the lingering echo of the last confused perceptions.

The distinct perceptions of sensible things are bound together by memory, which is an imitation of reason.

Rational perceptions are linked together by a law superior to that of memory; this law of the intelligence rests on two principles, which are the basis of all reasoning, the principle of the *sufficient reason,* and the principle of *contradiction.*

By the principle of the sufficient reason we judge that no fact can take place without a reason sufficient for its occurring so rather than otherwise. This principle is the basis of all theories which have facts for their object.

By the principle of contradiction we judge everything to be false which implies at once affirmation and negation: which comes to the same thing as taking for true everything which is contained in a notion, that is to say, all notions identical with it. The principle of contradiction is, therefore, at bottom the principle of identity. It is the basis of all theories which have necessary truths for their object.

As the principle of the sufficient reason supposes facts to which it is applied, so the principle of contradiction supposes indemonstrable first truths, of which it effects the development. But, although these two principles are distinct, still, in as far as they correspond to two different orders of knowledge, the one is derived from the other. For the necessity of a sufficient reason for the existence of every fact is itself a necessary truth, the negative of which would imply a contradiction. The principle of contradiction is therefore the root of all the sciences; it constitutes the unity of the human mind.

Thus far the human mind has only a subjective or logical unity. But it can advance thereby to an objective unity, that is to say, it can find not only the principle of knowledge, but also the principle even of things. It is true, indeed, that, in ascending the series of contingent facts, the sufficient reason of each particular fact is found in an anterior fact, this will nevertheless not give the sufficient reason for the existence of the whole series. The principle of the sufficient reason, followed to its last extent, obliges us to predicate the ultimate reason of all facts in a substance not contingent, but necessary. In the same way, if necessary eternal truths have any reality, this reality must also have existence in a substance necessary as themselves. If the necessary being does not exist, there are neither necessary truths, nor, *à fortiori*, contingent things. We cannot deny his existence without denying all existence; without falling, consequently, into the greatest contradictions.

Thus the principle of the sufficient reason leads us to acknowledge the ultimate reason of all contingent things. The principle of contradiction leads us to an eternal sphere of essences. The being who is at once the source of existences and the substance of truth, is God; for this being possesses absolute perfection, which is but the exclusion of all limitation. As he is the reason of the whole series of contingent things, he cannot be limited at any gradation of that series. Nor can a principle of limitation for him any more be found in the region of necessary truths; for necessity, so far from excluding in any degree existence, necessarily involves it. In a word, the idea of the supremely perfect Being, free from all limitations, implies his existence. If he did not exist, he would be at the same time possible and impossible; possible, since we have the idea of him; impossible, since his non-existence could have no other reason than just the impossibility of his existence. From the fact that the notion of the Supreme Being is not contradictory, we must therefore conclude that he exists. God is the being whose logical possibility implies his actual existence. Here Leibnitz falls in with the demonstration of Descartes. Although he pretended that his proof *à priori* of the existence of God was an improvement upon that of

Descartes, we cannot perceive any fundamental difference.

Arrived at God, the human mind comes into the possession of objective unity. It has found the prime monad, the unity of unities, to which he can thenceforward attach the whole theory of the universe. The monads are produced by perpetual *flashings* (as of lightning) of the infinite monad, which are limited by the *receptivity* of creatures. That which exists in created monads, exists without limits in the uncreated monad. There is in God a power which is the source of all beings, as there exists in monads a principle of activity which is the source of all their modes of being. There is in God an intelligence which contains the *schema* of ideas, as there is in the monads a *schema* which determines their own peculiar character. There is in God a good-will which is moved by the motive of the greatest good, as there is in the monads an internal appetency which makes them pass from one state to another state, and which is also a natural tendency towards their greatest good.

The general theory of the universe should afford a solution of two problems, which, in the times of Leibnitz especially, were agitated by the most powerful minds. The universe may be considered in its relations with God, and in the relations of creatures to each other. Compared with the infinite being, is the universe, or total collection of finite beings, destitute of infinite perfection solely from the nature of things, or is it, besides, destitute of any degree of finite perfection? This is the first of the problems. Leibnitz replied to it by optimism. Compared among themselves, do creatures exert upon each other a reciprocal influence? This is the second problem. The Cartesian philosophy sought the solution of it in the theory of occasional causes: Leibnitz substituted the theory of pre-established harmony.

In respect to the first question, Leibnitz aimed first to establish optimism by deduction from the very notion of God. God, who is absolute perfection, can have been moved in the act of creation only by the relative perfection possible in creatures. He has not, therefore, in his wisdom preferred a world more remote from absolute perfection to a world that approached nearer to it. But Leibnitz did not limit himself to the *à priori* proof of optimism; he endeavoured also to verify his system *à posteriori*, by reconciling the existence of evil with the existence of the most perfect world.

Evil may be considered in its possibility and in its actual existence. The possibility of evil makes necessarily a part of the creation, because it is derived from the limitation of creatures. Considered in its actual existence, evil is divided into metaphysical, physical, and moral evil. Metaphysical evil, which is only the very imperfection of creatures, must subsist in the most perfect world, since created things are not susceptible of infinite perfection, which is peculiar to God.—Physical evil or pain is a superior order of good, a moral good, in as far as it is the punishment of moral evil; it is also, in the mere sphere of enjoyment, often the principle of a greater good; and in all cases there is nothing to prove that it does not actually receive, or will not one day receive, a superabundant compensation; from whence it follows that in its sum total it cannot be affirmed that pain is not a good.—Moral evil or sin is not, indeed, like metaphysical evil, an absolute necessity of creation; it is not in itself, like physical evil, an efficient means of the greatest good, but its permission may be the condition of the greatest good; or, in other terms, nothing authorizes us to affirm that the perfection of the world, that is, the manifestation of the perfections of God in the world, did not require that God should permit this effect of the free-will of man. But if it be true that this was requisite, God not only could, but, moreover, must permit it, since he could have prevented it only by committing evil himself, in the very fact of preferring, by a choice unworthy of his wisdom, a less perfect to the most perfect world.

We pass to the relations of creatures to each other. The Cartesian philosophy had been led to the system of occasional causes by the impossibility of conceiving that the extended substance could act upon the thinking substance, and vice versâ. This difficulty did not exist in the philosophy of Leibnitz, who recognised but one sole kind of substance. But another difficulty presented itself: Leibnitz had maintained in principle that the monads could not act upon each other, inasmuch as they were essentially simple. How then to conceive the correlation which manifests itself between what takes place in one state and what takes place in another state, for instance, between the mind and the body with which it is united? It is very true, replied Leibnitz, that there is no physical connexion between the monads, but there is an ideal connexion. Their relations are contained in the divine ideas; and God, in creating a monad, predetermined its relations with other monads. He regulated in the beginning the internal principle of its variations in such a way that all the evolutions of the principle should concur with the evolutions that were to take place in other monads. The beings that we call spirits, that is, monads endowed with self-consciousness, and the beings that we call bodies, that is, aggregations of simple monads, act solely according to their own internal force; the former as if there were no bodies in existence, the latter as if there were no spirits in existence. But, in virtue of the pre-established harmony, the corporeal world and the spiritual world are like two clocks, which, though reciprocally independent, mark simultaneously the same hours, in consequence of an internal mechanism in which the clockmaker has realized his own ideas.

It is to be conceived that in this system, where each monad acts by itself without being modified by another, the distinction of active and passive is not real, but only phenomenal. It has its foundation, not in the objects, but in our mode of conceiving them. We say that one being is passive relatively to another being supposed active, when we use that which is distinctly known to us in the latter in order to conceive the sufficient reason of what takes place in the former.

Leibnitz not only considered the hypothesis of pre-established harmony as the most satisfactory explanation of the phenomena of the correlation of substances, but, moreover, he saw in it a consequence of his system of optimism. The perfection of the universe requires the best order of combination, or the most complete unity with the most extended variety. The evolutions of each monad being adapted to the evolutions of all the others, a more perfect unity of plan cannot be conceived. But, at the same time, each monad, by its harmony with all the others, reflecting in its own point of view the whole universe, there results from it the greatest possible variety. Just as a city seen from different points receives optically a multiplied existence, so the universe, though essentially one, is multiplied by the different points of view furnished by the innumerable monads.

The general consequence of all the foregoing principles is, on the one hand, that everything is animated, since nothing exists but monads essentially active; and, on the other hand, that each monad, representative of all nature, according to a mode of perception more or less developed, is constantly modified by its internal activity, as if it received the echo of everything that passes in the universe to the farthest limits of creation. This life, one and universal, is, in the view of Leibnitz, a magnificent con firmation of his optimist doctrine.

But in the bosom of that unity, bodies and spirits act according to laws which are specific to them; the first observing the laws of efficient causes, the second the laws of final causes.

By the general principles of his theory of bodies, Leibnitz combated at once Descartes and Newton. We have seen already how he attacked the bases of the Cartesian physics. As to Newton, who, through the medium of Clarke, maintained a controversy with Leibnitz, the principal points of separation were relative to the most general cosmological notions. Newton had maintained the existence of a vacuum: Leibnitz asserted that there was no sufficient reason for a vacuum; for the more there is of matter in the universe, the more the power and wisdom of God are exercised. Newton considered space as a reality; he supposed beyond the material world a space without limits. Leibnitz replied, that if space were anything real in itself, it would doubtless be infinite and eternal, and so would be God; which would be contradictory, since space is divisible, and God is absolutely one and simple. Space, in the view of the German philosopher, was nothing but a relation, like time. Time is the sphere of successions, space the sphere of coexistences. Finally, Newton had concluded from physical theories that the forces of nature would be gradually exhausted, and that the moment would come when God would stretch forth again his creative hand to repair the universe. Leibnitz replied that it would not do to represent God as a feeble or ignorant author of machines that may need repairs.

By the side of his physical cosmology Leibnitz laid down the bases of a sort of moral cosmology, which also contained the foundations of politics. Spirits, which differ from inferior monads in that the latter represent only the universe, while the former represent God himself, form, together with him, a perfect state, of which he is the monarch. All sociality has its source in resemblance to God.

The universal law of this state of intelligences is love. Love unites beings to each other and to God, without destroying the propensity which leads each one to seek his own individual gratification; for love is the pleasure one takes in the happiness of another: justice is enlightened love.

But in order to demonstrate that the honesty and justice which secure the interest of all are in harmony with utility or the interest of each, it is necessary to take in the universal sphere, to carry our thoughts up to God, and from this height to discover beyond this life a future life, where the divine plan shall be accomplished.

Observations.

1. Bacon had traced a method, but had occupied himself much less with the explanation of things. Leibnitz devoted himself much more to the explanation of things than to the method to be followed in order to arrive at it. Descartes embraced at once method and the explanation of things.

2. We have pointed out how, in certain respects,

the philosophy of Leibnitz was a reaction against that of Bacon, in other respects against that of Descartes. It is necessary to take this double point of view in order to form an exact idea of it.

3. Considered as a whole, this philosophy aimed at combining in the highest degree unity and variety. The notion that Leibnitz formed of perception, the source of all knowledge, made him incessantly strive to obtain this result, since perception, as he conceived it, was the representation of variety in unity. Philosophy, which was in some sort perception in the large, should accordingly produce this representation in the vastest proportions.

4. The theories of Leibnitz contain the principles of idealism. Material substance is at bottom only a pure phenomenon: the action and reaction of beings upon each other is only a simple conception of the mind. All ideas are only the product of the development of the monad.

5. The system of pre-established harmony attacks the common notion of the union of mind and body. It divides the universe into two worlds, whose apparent union implies their real and absolute separation.

6. The philosophy of Leibnitz contains, however, some portions that are admirable. It represents one of the essential elements of the human mind, the ideal, as the philosophy of Bacon represents the other, the sensible element.

7. The influence of the philosophy of Leibnitz was felt in nearly the whole German philosophy of his epoch, to which he gave an inclination towards idealism, which showed itself at first in two forms, mystic idealism and rational idealism. Those of the German philosophers who, while professing doctrines opposed under certain aspects to the idealism of Leibnitz, embraced under other aspects a mystic ideal

ism, are particularly represented by Christian Thomasius. The other philosophers, who were the continuators of the Leibnitzian philosophy, are represented by Wolff, the most celebrated of the disciples of Leibnitz.

THOMASIUS.

CHRISTIAN THOMASIUS, whose father had been the master of Leibnitz, was born at Leipsic in 1655, and died at Halle in 1728.

The fundamental doctrine of Thomasius presents a singular combination, the union of sensualism and mysticism.

Thomasius had felt that it was impossible to deduce all truths from sensations, and, above all, the highest truths, those of religion and morality. On the other hand, in the analysis of the intelligence it seemed to him that it never operated but upon a stock furnished by sensation. In this point of view it is necessary either to deny the truths not contained in sensations, or to find in the human mind a source of knowledge distinct from sensation. Thomasius held that it was false to say man was in relation with truth only by his intellect; he maintained that the human mind had in some sort two organs to apprehend truth, the intellect and the will. We attain possession of truth either by the view of the mind or by the inclination of the soul. Sensation is the principle of all the rational notions upon which the intellect operates; love is the principle of the truths of sentiment. By this theory Thomasius, leaving one half of philosophy in sensualism, carried the other half into mysticism, by admitting a perception of the true radically independent of the intelligence.

The distinction of active and passive plays a great

part in the conceptions of Thomasius. The intellect and the will are sometimes active and sometimes passive. These two states correspond to different principles. The passive state attests the presence of a blind, dark, cold, corruptible principle; this is matter. The active state comes from a luminous, vital, energetic, incorruptible principle; this is of the nature of spirit.

For the rest, though Thomasius treated of the various branches of philosophy, yet he chiefly devoted himself to the task of reducing to theory morals and the science of rights.

WOLFF.

CHRISTIAN WOLFF, born at Breslau in 1679, died in 1764, was the correspondent and friend of Leibnitz. After the death of his master he was considered the first philosopher of Germany. He contributed powerfully to destroy the empire of the peripatetic philosophy in the schools.

Wolff was in general only a continuator of the philosophy of Leibnitz; but he added much less to it in the way of substance than of form.

1. He endeavoured to combine and arrange all the views scattered in the works of Leibnitz, by referring that immense mass of ideas to some simple principles. The kind of unity established by Wolff consisted, however, far more in a methodical exposition of ideas than in their intimate logical connexion. In this respect he scarcely went beyond what had been done by Leibnitz.

2. He applied to the exposition of this philosophy the processes of the geometrical method, and considered all truths as sustaining to each other relations analogous to those that exist between numbers.

3. He attempted to form a sort of statistics of

philosophical problems, and of the solutions which they might receive. He undertook in this respect a labour of nomenclature and classification analogous to that of Bacon, but from a point of view different from that of the empirical philosopher.

4. He distinguished empirical reason, relating to the elements furnished by sensation, from pure reason, which perceives necessary truths.

5. As a consequence of this distinction, he asserted for ontology the importance denied to it by Bacon.

Observations.

The doctrines of Leibnitz, defended and developed by Wolff and other philosophers of that period, encountered, particularly in Germany, numerous adversaries, who may be ranged around Crusius as their centre. But their attacks did not destroy the predominating influence of those doctrines, which led the way in some degree to the philosophy of Kant. The distinction between empirical and pure reason opened the point of view at which Kant took his position. On the other hand, Thomasius, in denying to the intellect relatively to religious and moral truths the authority which he accorded to sentiment, or inclination of the soul, preluded the conception of Kant, who allowed to the practical reason a validity denied by him to the speculative reason. There is undoubtedly a great difference between the theory of the one respecting the practical reason, and the theory of the other respecting truths perceived by love; yet, spite of this difference, a certain analogy subsists between them. We shall soon see how the system of Kant bore the impress of the threefold influence of the schools of Bacon, of Descartes, and of Leibnitz. However, by reason of his eminently idealist character, he was not an emanation of the school of Leibnitz, but a result of the intellectual habits which the philosophy of Leibnitz had propagated in Germany.

SECOND PART.

GERMAN SCHOOLS.

KANT.

Historical Notices.

EMMANUEL KANT was born at Königsberg in 1724. He there went through the University course. After having been for some time a tutor in private families, he attained to the chair of logic and metaphysics, and afterwards the rectorship in his University. There is nothing striking in the external events and circumstances of his history; his life was in a sort altogether internal. He died in 1804. The most celebrated of his works is his *Critique of Pure Reason*, which he published in 1781, and in which he laid down the principles of the philosophical reformation he had undertaken to establish. He developed and applied these principles in numerous other writings, among which may be named, the *Prolegomena to Metaphysics*, *Critique of Practical Reason*, *Critique of Judgment*, *Metaphysical Principles of the Science of Right*, and an *Essay on Anthopology*.

Exposition.

Setting out with the principles of the empirical philosophy, Hume had shaken the foundations of human knowledge. Kant demanded if it were true, as that philosopher took for granted, that human knowledge is composed solely of elements furnished by experience, if there were not, on the contrary, notions independent of sensation, and produced by the understanding alone. He noticed, in the first place, that the mathematical sciences imply notions of this kind. The judgment by which we pronounce the radii of a circle equal is not founded upon experience; for this judgment affirms something necessary, while experience gives us nothing but simply facts; it affirms something universal, while experience gives us nothing but particular facts. Besides empirical cognitions or knowledge *à posteriori*, there exists, then, cognitions *à priori*, originally distinct from any sensible element. Struck with the character of the mathematical principles, Kant afterward inquired whether the entire system of cognitions did not rest upon judgments marked with the same character, and, in that case, what is the source of those judgments, and what are the conditions and limits of their legitimate application.

He attempted to determine in the most precise manner the fundamental problem of the human mind, by considering that there were two sorts of judgments. In the one the attribute or predicate is contained in the subject, as, for example, *The infinitely perfect Being is good.* Such judgments do nothing but develop a notion without adding to it any other notions, and in this sense they do not enlarge the circle of our knowledge. Kant gave them the name of analytical judgments. But there are other judgments where the attribute is not contained in the subject, as, for example, *Every phenomenon has a principle or cause.* The idea of principle or cause is not contained in the simple notion of phenomenon. Such judgments increase our knowledge, in that they consist in the affirmation of something not comprised in the conception of the subject. Kant called them synthetic judgments.

Combining, then, the distinction of analytical and synthetic judgments with the distinction of knowledge *à posteriori* and knowledge *à priori*, he remarked, first, that all analytical judgments are *à priori*, since it is not necessary to have recourse to experience in order to affirm the relation of attribute to subject, when this relation is contained in the very conception of the subject. But, at the same time, he believed he ascertained that of synthetic judgments some are *à posteriori* and others *à priori*. When I say, *All bodies are heavy*, I form a synthetic judgment *à posteriori*; the attribute *heavy* is not contained in the conception of the subject *body*; their relation is furnished only by experience. But, on the contrary, this other synthetic judgment, *Every phenomenon has a principle or a cause*, is *à priori*, for experience gives only the simple phenomenon.

This established, we see what, according to Kant, is the radical problem of the human mind. There is no difficulty in conceiving the possibility of synthetic judgments *à posteriori*, for this synthesis is only the expression of experience. Nor is it difficult to conceive that analytical judgments should be *à priori*, for they are only the expression of what is contained in the conception of the subject. But how to conceive the possibility of synthetic judgments *à priori*? In these judgments the relation of the attribute to the subject is neither given by the conception of the subject, as in analytical judgments *à priori*, nor by experience, as in synthetic judgments *à posteriori*. Upon what foundation, then, do they rest? To solve this problem Kant undertook a general criticism of the grounds of human knowledge. His speculations are divided into three principal branches: criticism of *theoretical* reason; criticism of *practical* reason; and, lastly, criticism of a third mode of reason, whose office it is to establish the alliance of the theoretical and practical reason.

Criticism of the Theoretical Reason.

The mind is affected by impressions, which may be designated by the general name of sensations, because, whatever be their cause, internal or external, they are perceived by man in as far as he is a sensitive being. They produce in the mind a representation which may be called *intuition*. The aptitude of the mind to be affected by them is called receptivity.

In the sensibility or receptivity it is necessary to distinguish between the matter and the form. The elements furnished by experience are the *matter*. But these elements all fall within the framework of the notions of time and space. These notions are not given by experience, for we can suppose all the objects of sensation may be annihilated; on that supposition the notions of time and space are still more the less inherent in the mind. These notions *à priori* are then the *forms* of the receptivity.

But the simple sensibility which receives intuitions does not suffice to produce ideas, for an intuition and an idea are different things. When I see a house, I receive at first a variety of impressions corresponding to the different parts of the object perceived; but the idea of the house is not formed until the mind has combined these intuitions in the unity of consciousness. The formation of ideas supposes, then, in addition to the passive receptivity, an active intervention of the understanding, which may be designated by the term spontaneity.

But this is only the first act of cognition. After having united intuitions in order to form ideas, the understanding also recalls the idea of unity in order to produce judgments. Ideas are the matter of judgments; but, besides the matter of judgments, there are also the forms which constitute them by being applied to the matter. All judgments are referable:

Either to *quantity:* judgments are then either individual, or particular, or universal;

Or to *quality:* judgments are then either affirmative, or negative, or limitative;

Or to *relation:* judgments are then either categorical, or hypothetical, or disjunctive;

Or to *modality:* to which belong judgments problematical, assertory, and necessary.

The four fundamental modes of judgments give the following categories:

Quantity . . .	Unity. Plurality. Universality.
Quality . . .	Reality. Negation. Limitation.
Relation . . .	Substance and accident. Causality and dependance. Action and reaction.
Modality . . .	Possibility, impossibility. Existence, non-existence. Necessity, contingence.

All notions fall within the framework of these categories, as all intuitions fall under the notions of time and space. These categories are not furnished by experience; they are the universal and necessary laws of the understanding. They are its forms, as time and space are the forms of the sensibility.

The production of judgments corresponds to the production of ideas. Just as intuitions are the matter of ideas, ideas are the matter of judgments. The spontaneity of the understanding reduces intuitions to unity, under the *à priori* conditions of time and space, expressed by the categories.

But human knowledge implies still an ulterior unity. The judgments are in their turn brought to unity. The act which produces this unity is reasoning, the faculty which operates in reasoning is called reason, to distinguish it from the understanding, inasmuch as the latter word is relative solely to the formation of judgments and ideas.

In all reasoning the conclusion depends on the premises: the letter contain the particular condition of the former. But if the premises themselves have particular conditions, they are nothing but conclusions, for which premises must be sought until we arrive at the totality of conditions, that is, to the absolute condition. The office of reason is therefore to seek for that condition, to establish the greatest possible unity of judgments. Now, as there are three general forms of reasoning, the categorical, hypothetical, and disjunctive, there are three ideas, which establish for each form of reasoning the absolute condition of unity.

Reasoning is categorical when the understanding furnishes to the reason judgments in which the attribute is considered as residing in the subject. Reason should, then, seek for the idea of a subject which does not itself reside in any other: this idea is the idea of substance.

Reasoning is hypothetical when the attribute of judgments is united to a subject only in virtue of a particular supposition. Reason should seek, then, for an absolute hypothesis; and as no particular phenomenon can give it, this absolute hypothesis is perhaps only the absolute totality of all phenomena, that is, the idea of the whole series of facts which compose the universe.

Finally, reasoning is disjunctive when it refers to judgments where the predicate is united to the subject as a part of a whole. But a whole can itself be only a part of a larger whole, and thus on till we come to an absolute whole, which allows of making a complete or absolute division of all the parts. Reason, in order to work out this division, must therefore seek for the idea of a being which comprehends all existences, or the idea of the Supreme Being.

Now experience can furnish neither of these three radical ideas, on which depends in the last analysis the unity of judgments, which is the aim of reason. It cannot furnish the ontological idea of substance, for experience corresponds only to phenomena. It cannot furnish the cosmological idea of the absolute totality of phenomena; for, however large the number of facts observed, the number is limited, and represents nothing absolute. Lastly, it cannot give the theological idea of the being that contains all existences, since particular existences are the sole objects of experience.

Consequently, the notions by which reason constitutes the unity of judgments are *à priori*, as also the notions by means of which the understanding constitutes the unity of ideas, as also the notions by means of which it brings intuitions to unity. Reason, considered with respect to the notions which are its forms, is pure reason.

From these principles Kant concluded:

1. That human knowledge, taken in general, is composed of two elements, the empirical or *à posteriori* element, and the *à priori* element, which is derived from the intelligence. If the intelligence did not apply its forms to the intuitions produced by sensation, the intuitions would never become cognitions. But without the intuitions, without the data of experience, the forms of the intelligence would be empty forms, they would be inapplicable, they would be without employment.

2. That all the notions of the pure reason are destitute of objective reality, or, rather, that we have no right to attribute to them such a reality, because reason does not operate upon the intuitions, but only upon the forms of the judgments which the understanding has produced.

3. That we make an illegitimate use of reason when, attributing to these notions an objective reality, we would thereby apprehend existences which are not contained in the sphere of the sensible world. We would go beyond the limits of human knowledge, which are just the limits of experience.

4. That we equally violate the laws of the human mind when, instead of using the notions of reason solely to systematize our judgments, we would apply them immediately to the data of experience. This abuse produces the antinomies, that is, series of judgments which terminate in contradictory results: antinomies, which should apprize us that the attempt from which they result is radically vicious.

5. Lastly, that what we call the laws of nature are nothing but the laws of our own intelligence, which imposes them upon nature, or, in other words, that the order which we attribute to things is at bottom only the order of our perceptions, determined by the constituent forms of our intelligence.

This system evidently conducts to consequences destructive of religion. If, in fact, all human cognitions are contained within the circle of experience, the ideas of God, of the future life, and all those which flow therefrom, are ideas without real validity. Kant admitted that this consequence was an inevitable corollary of his criticism of the speculative reason; but he distinguished in man another reason, which he called practical, and which gave, according to him, a solid foundation for beliefs, which the speculative reason was unable to establish.

Criticism of the Practical Reason.

The object of speculative reason is the resolution of this question: What can I know? But man also asks another question: What ought I to do? In as far as it goes to solve this question, reason is practical: it seeks the determining principles of the will; and, as reason necessarily tends to unity, it seeks here also an absolute principle.

Among the determining principles of the will should be distinguished, as in the theoretical principles, two elements, the one material, the other formal. The material element is composed of all the motives which act upon the sensibility, all the motives of enjoyment; the formal element comprehends disinterested motives, or motives relative, not to the sensibility, but to the pure reason. The first contain nothing universal and necessary; the second alone can furnish the absolute principle of determination. Now, as soon as sensible motives are put aside, nothing can be conceived as the principle of determination but that rule which alone is absolute, or independent of every particular condition: *Act according to a maxim which would admit of being regarded as a general law for all acting beings.* This Kant calls the categorical imperative.

But this absolute principle of the practical reason is bound up with three theoretical principles or postulates, without which it could not be conceived: the postulate of freedom, the postulate of the immortality of the soul, the postulate of the existence of God.

1. If man be not free, he could attribute his determinations only to his propensities, that is, to that which corresponds to the sensibility: therefore the absolute principle of the practical reason implies liberty.

2. The principle of the practical reason, as an absolute rule, commands man to establish a perfect harmony between his intentions and the moral law; a harmony which constitutes holiness, or the ideal of virtue. Man should therefore tend towards this ideal; but its complete realization is not possible, because man is subject to the conditions of the sensibility, which relate not to the ideal of virtue, but to the empiricism of enjoyment. It is necessary, therefore, that man should strive to approach this ideal by a perpetual progress, and the possibility of this indefinite progress supposes the immortality of the soul.

3. Virtue is the supreme end. If happiness by itself were the supreme end, reasonable beings would not have had the faculty of self-determination; instinct would have sufficed. But, on the other hand, they are also formed with an invincible desire of hap piness. Now the harmony of virtue and of happiness cannot be established by man, because man, free in respect of his will, is dependant upon nature in respect of happiness, and nature itself does not accomplish this necessary harmony. Its realization therefore supposes a cause independent of nature, who both can and wills to produce this harmony, who is consequently endowed with intelligence and will. This sovereign cause is God.

The ideas of freedom, of immortality, of the existence of God, have, according to Kant, as postulates of the practical reason, an objective validity, which they cannot obtain from the theoretical reason. The practical reason, determining actions, commands real effects; now it would be absurd that real effects should be produced by principles which were not themselves real.

Criticism of the Judgment.

The theoretical reason furnishes the laws of nature, the practical reason furnishes the laws of freedom. They have both their peculiar principles, which would remain constantly separate without a particular faculty, by which man could apply to the world of nature the conceptions of the world of freedom. The principle according to which this faculty operates is the agreement or fitness of means to ends; an agreement which exists in the actions of free beings, and which we can transfer into the actions of nature by conceiving the union of nature with the freedom which acts in it and by it.

The faculty which serves as the bond between the speculative and the practical sphere is called by Kant the faculty of *Judgment.* This denomination has some inconveniences, because it is employed in a different sense in the criticism of the theoretical reason.

Leaving this out of view, however, the faculty of *judging* (as now conceived) has two modes. When it considers the concurrence of means in the forms of things in such a way as to produce a sentiment of pleasure, it is *esthetical;* when it considers this concurrence under a purely logical point of view, in order to obtain the simple knowledge of things, without any regard to the sentiment of pleasure, it is *teleological.*

The criticism of the *esthetic* judgment is the theory of the beautiful and sublime. Both are purely subjective. The beautiful is the consciousness of being able easily to bring a variety, which the imagination represents to us, to one idea of the understanding: it is the sentiment of the harmony which exists between these two faculties. As this sentiment is the sentiment of our own power, it is accompanied with satisfaction. The sublime, on the contrary, is the consciousness of our inability to embrace by the imagination ideas which the reason presents to us. The sentiment of this disproportion is accompanied with a kind of sadness, because it apprizes us in one relation of our weakness; but in another relation it exalts us, because we feel ourselves superior by our reason to the world of sensible things.

The criticism of the *teleological* judgment contains the theory of nature, according to the principle of final causes, or the relation of means to ends, appli ed not to the forms, but to the constitution of things. It considers beings as organized to attain certain particular ends, and each special organization as a dependance of a general organization of nature, in which particular ends are only the means of a supreme and universal end. Here the criticism of the teleological judgment results in the religious ideas, of which the practical reason had demonstrated the reality.

Observations.

In order to a right apprehension of the character of the philosophy of Kant, it should be compared with the three great schools founded by Descartes, Bacon, and Leibnitz.

1. Like Descartes, Kant made psychology the basis of philosophy. But Descartes, after having at the outset concentrated his mind upon the contemplation of the thinking *me*, attempted immediately to pass outward, and by the notion of God to connect the speculations of reason with an external reality, the source of all reality. Kant, on the contrary, fundamentally destroyed all relation between speculation and external realities; he confined himself

within an order of ideas purely subjective, from whence he could not come out, even by his theory of practical reason, but by doing violence to the principles established in his theory of speculative reason. By attributing to the practical reason a validity which he denied to the speculative, he fell into a radical inconsistency, since the practical reason had its basis necessarily in ideas borrowed from the speculative reason.

2. The philosophy of Kant, while fundamentally separated from the sensualism of the school of Bacon, came near to it, nevertheless, in its consequences. Three sorts of sensualism may be distinguished. There is a sensualism which maintains at once sensation as the sole principle of knowledge, and the sensible world as the sole sphere in which the intelligence can exercise itself. This is complete sensualism. There is another sensualism, which, while setting out from sensation, pretends to deduce from it the knowledge of realities distinct from sensible objects. Lastly, there are theories sensualist in their results, in the sense that they deny to man the possibility of *knowing* realities lying beyond the senses, though they admit, in the formation of human knowledge, a principle distinct from sensation, but which can apply itself only to elements furnished by sensation itself. Such is the foundation of the doctrine of Kant, although he attempted to escape this result in the practical sphere by the inconsistency that has just been noticed.

3. The idealist tendency of the philosophy of Leibnitz is evidently reproduced in the theories of Kant. According to Leibnitz, the knowledge of nature and its laws is produced by the purely internal development of the soul. According to Kant, the soul imposes upon nature its own laws. But Leibnitz ad-

mitted that the soul is representative of external reality: Kant denied this representation. On the one hand, all ideas *à priori* are merely simple forms of the intelligence; on the other hand, intuitions teach us nothing of the nature of things. All that man can affirm is that he is placed in a world of appearances, which he combines according to the laws of his reason.

4. The influence of the philosophy of Kant is due particularly to two causes. First, it had, as we have seen, its roots in the three great anterior philosophies; secondly, it pretended to supply their insufficiency by determining, from a complete criticism of the reason, which had been partially attempted by Descartes, the laws according to which the sensualist principle, represented by Bacon, and the idealist principle, represented by Leibnitz, should be combined without overpassing their respective limits.

Continuation of the Philosophical Movement in Germany.

While many German writers defended, with *Herder*, the empirical philosophy against Kantism, and while others, with *Eberhard* and *Platner*, maintained many of the Leibnitzian doctrines, Kantism provoked two opposite results: the one was a reaction, represented by *Jacobi;* the other was a development, represented by *Reinhold*, and, above all, by *Fichte.*

JACOBI.

Fred. Henry Jacobi, who was born in 1743 and died in 1804, maintained that all rationalistic philosophy resulted either in pantheism if it was dogmatical, or in skepticism, at least in respect to everything connected with religious or moral truth, if it confined itself within the limits of criticism as established by Kant. Instead of taking reason as the basis of human knowledge, he substituted sentiment, which reveals to us in an immediate manner, instinctive and independent of all rational conception, both the sensible world and the moral and religious world. Sentiment, which is originally a pure belief, destitute of all proof, produces in its development all the elements of which human reason is composed.

On the other hand, *Leonard Reinhold* (born in 1759, died in 1825) pretended to complete the work of Kant, and believed he had given him the unity which he was accused of wanting, by reducing all parts of his system to a single principle, consciousness considered as the representative faculty. He devoted himself particularly to describing the characteristics of this fundamental faculty.

FICHTE.

BUT it was chiefly Fichte who developed the Kantian philosophy. JOHN THEOPHILUS FICHTE, born in Lusatia in 1762, succeeded Reinhold in the philosophical chair at Jena, afterward professed the transcendental philosophy at Erlangen, and was finally appointed rector of the University of Berlin. He died in 1814. The substance of his philosophy is contained in his work on the *Fundamental Principles of all Scientific Doctrine.*

Exposition.

Kant had attempted to avoid absolute idealism by admitting that sensible intuitions correspond to external realities. Jacobi saw in this only an inconsistency, and predicted that Kantism would resolve itself into pure idealism. And, in point of fact, why was it that Kant refused to the conceptions of reason an objective validity? It was because this validity could not be demonstrated. But it is equally impossible to demonstrate the objective validity of sensible intuitions. They must, then, needs come to be considered likewise as simple subjective phenomena. Such was the point of view taken by Fichte. Accordingly, he held all realities to be only creations of the thinking principle, and all existence only thought itself.

In separating the fundamental conceptions of Fichte from the logical circumlocutions in which he has enveloped them, and which involve them in great obscurity, we may, it seems to us, reduce his views to the following principles:

1. The me first posits itself in an absolute and unlimited manner by an act of pure free-will.

2. It is of the essence of the me to fall back upon itself in reflection. It is at once subject and object.

3. The me cannot thus posit itself without determining itself by the not-me. For the me as *object* must appear in a certain relation as not-me to the me as *subject*.

4. In determining itself by the not-me, the me arrests its own activity; it becomes limited and divisible.

5. Then springs up the faculty of feeling, which is only the faculty of perception, the limitation of the free activity of the me.

6. From hence are derived all our notions of a twofold reality, of spirit and of the world, of freedom and of necessity.

7. The me, so far forth as will, recognises itself as independent of the universe and as acting upon it. So far forth as intelligence, it projects itself as dependant upon the universe and dependant upon its action.

In his work on the *Destination of Man*, Fichte deduces from his Doctrine of Science the necessity of belief or faith as the indispensable ground of all human activity.

[The foregoing indications are so brief, that it is thought best to subjoin a few observations, less, however, in the expectation of rendering Fichte's views generally intelligible, than as due to a system so celebrated in the history of philosophy.

Fichte's special object was to construct a system in which the matter and form of all science should be deduced from one and the same principle, and thus to solve the problem of the relation of ideas to their objects: a problem on which had always turned the everlasting conflict between idealism and realism. He would thus give to philosophy the systematic unity, with the want of which the system of Kant had been reproached.

Accordingly, he took for his starting-point a primitive act of the personal thinking self, from which he deduces consciousness itself, as well as all its phenomena.

The popular philosophy assumes the reality of external objects, and that the mind both acts upon them and is acted upon by them. But this leaves the essential contradiction between matter and spirit, and the possibility of this twofold action, unexplained. Fichte avoided the contradiction by making external or objective reality a mere limitation of the activity of the mind. The thinking principle posits itself as determined by the objective, and also as determining the objective. Hence we have, as a fact of consciousness, the conception of reality external to ourselves; but Fichte denies the veracity of consciousness; the conception is all the reality there is. When we conceive objects as external to ourselves, the mind merely removes a reality as out of itself, to transfer it as to something that is not itself. When we conceive external objects as acting upon our minds, it is merely the mind limiting its own activity, and positing the object as not ourselves, while in reality it is we ourselves that act, and not any real objects out of ourselves. Everything is thus reduced to two different aspects of one and the same essential fact; sometimes we conceive the mind as active and objects as passive, sometimes the reverse.

In order to find the ground of this self-limitation in the thinking principle, Fichte distinguishes between the thinking principle considered as activity and considered as intelligence. The absolute personal self is an infinite free activity, containing in its essential nature the impulse to action, production, or creation; but the actions of an active principle, even of an infinite one, must of necessity be special determinations of its activity, that is, limited and finite. The absolute thinking principle, by this limitation, is evolved as intelligence; this limitation appears to the intelligence as the not-self opposed to the self, as the finite opposed to the infinite; and it constitutes all the objective reality there is. Thus the finite self or intelligence, and the world, are both equally demonstrated, indeed, because both are products of the absolute active principle, the absolute self.

Thus all contradiction between spirit and matter is removed on the system of Fichte, but it is only by the destruction of the latter. The chasm between the infinite and finite is also removed, but it is by the absorption of the finite and of the infinite into consciousness, and of all into thought. All the reality in the universe is expressed in the single word I. Yet the whole system is built upon an assumption which is arbitrary and groundless; the absolute I of Fichte is contradictory and impossible. Besides, this primitive act of the thinking principle by which it absolutely posits itself, and the not-self as opposed to itself, is a fact not falling within the history of experience, and we are made to get it by a process which he calls intellectual intuition, which, in fact, is nothing but an hypothesis illegitimately imposed upon his theory.

Fichte, after having thus destroyed by his *speculative* idealism the belief in the reality of an external world, and left nothing but a concatenation of purely phenomenal illusions, endeavoured in his *moral* system to ground the truths requisite for morality upon our belief in conscience. The principle of morals is absolute obedience to conscience. His ethics were of ascetic strictness. Faith in conscience requires us to believe in the existence of a spiritual world, and even of a sensible world, and also in the possibility of realizing the ideal prescribed by duty.

God is merely the moral order of the universe, a conception to which the mind rises from the consciousness of duty. We need not conceive God as a distinct being by himself, intelligent and personal, and the cause of this moral order; and there are difficulties in the way of so conceiving him: by ascribing to him these attributes, we make him finite, like ourselves; and we have the notion of creation to explain, which cannot rationally be done.

The supreme good is gained in the world of moral order by virtue. The supreme good is not happiness, which does not and cannot exist.

These views, unfolded in a paradoxical spirit, were considered a sort of atheism. They are inconsistent with all proper ideas of God; and, though Fichte did not admit this, yet he afterward renounced them. He varied his modes of expression, indeed, and even his doctrines, in his later writings. He had set out at first with the activity of the thinking principle; in the later form of his doctrine, he set out with the absolute existence of God as the sole reality and the sole life. In its first form, his doctrine was atheistical; in the second, pantheistical. The philosophy of Schelling seems to have contributed to this change of ideas.]

Skeptical Reaction against Kant.

Before complete idealism had been introduced by Fichte in the school of Kant, a skeptical reaction had been excited against Kantism. The philosophy of Kant had announced the pretension of establishing upon an immovable basis the structure of human knowledge, and of sapping the foundations of skepticism. A philosopher (G. E. Schulze), under the name Ænesidemus, undertook to show, on the contrary, that it could do nothing but confirm the skeptical philosophy, because, after destroying the bases admitted by anterior systems, it substituted nothing more solid in their place; and that the demonstrations with which it pretended to replace the gratuitous assertions of other philosophers, were themselves at bottom only assertions equally devoid of proof.

[ENGLISH PHILOSOPHY IN THE PERIOD BETWEEN LOCKE AND REID.

BEFORE proceeding to an exposition of the principles of the Scottish school, so called, of which the founder and chief representative is Reid, it seems proper to interpose, in addition to what has been said of Hume and Berkeley, some farther remarks on the progress of English philosophy in the interval between Locke and Reid.

It has already been seen how, in the seventeenth century, the moral consequences of Hobbes's empiricism produced a reaction represented by Cudworth and others.

The publication of Locke's Essay on the Understanding was followed by a rapid development of skepticism, materialism, and atheism. Opposition to his system was not, however, wanting; it was early assailed in behalf of religion by Henry Lee and John Norris; also by Bishops Stillingfleet and Brown; and its defects were pointed out by Shaftesbury, in his Letters of a Nobleman to a Young Man at the University.

Among those who turned the principles of Hobbes and Locke against the received doctrines of religion and morals was William Coward, who wrote several treatises against the immateriality of the soul. He was combated by Turner and Brughton. The natural mortality of the soul was likewise maintained by Henry Dodwell. Anthony Collins, a friend and pupil of Locke, applied the principles of his master to skeptical and infidel conclusions, combating the freedom of man and the evidences of Christianity. Against these two latter, and particularly Collins, numerous adversaries appeared, among the most eminent of whom was the celebrated Dr. Samuel Clarke, who vigorously opposed the new doctrines of Hobbes and Locke. Maintaining a necessary harmony between revealed religion and reason, he attempted to furnish a new demonstration of the Being and Attributes of God. He held space and time to be attributes of a substance; and as they are necessarily conceived as infinite, so likewise must be the subject of them. That infinite substance is God. He deduced the immortality of the soul from the idea of immaterial being.

Systems of Disinterested Morals.

But it was chiefly against the ethical system of Hobbes and Locke that the reaction of the English mind was directed. There arose a series of writers, who combated the selfish system with great ability, and maintained a disinterested morality, seeking at the same time to demonstrate the fundamental truths of morals, independently of revelation, by the method of psychological observation. They have shed great light upon the facts of man's moral constitution, and incidentally upon the origin of ideas and the mental faculties in general. These writers contributed very powerfully to check the progress of exclusive sensualism; to prevent such a development as it received in France; and to prepare the way for the more systematic labours of Reid.

But while these writers all agree in maintaining, in opposition to the selfish system, that our moral ideas cannot be resolved into sensations, and that the motive of moral action is disinterested, they differ from each other as to the principle of morals. One class refers our moral ideas to a sentiment or instinct which has its basis in a special faculty, termed sometimes the moral faculty, conscience, or, more strictly in conformity with their views, the *moral sense.* The other class refers our moral ideas to reason. To the first class belong Shaftesbury, Butler, and Hutcheson; to the second, Wollaston, Clarke, and Price.

Intermediate between these is a class of writers who resolve our moral ideas into some form of instinctive sentiment, but not to a special moral sense of these are Hume and Adam Smith.

Systems of the Moral Sense.

Anthony Ashley Cooper, Earl of SHAFTESBURY, was born in 1671. Obliged by his delicate health to retire from public affairs, he devoted his leisure to philosophy and letters. He died in 1713.

Shaftesbury was the first philosopher who professed this system, and the first who introduced into the language of philosophy the term *moral sense.*

He divided our desires into two distinct classes: benevolent or social, and personal affections. Affections of the first class prompt us instinctively to love the happiness of others for its own sake. The approbation we feel for conduct conformed to the benevolent affections is distinct in its nature from any reference to our own personal advantage. It is referable to the moral sense, which is a special faculty and a distinct part of our constitution, as much as our external senses are special faculties appropriated respectively to the apprehension of their special objects. The office of the moral sense is to apprehend and approve moral good, and to feel obligation. The affections of our nature which are agreeable to this sense are, on that account, morally good; the contrary, morally bad. In our constitution, the moral sense is superior to the outward senses; the benevolent to the personal affections. Virtue consists in giving them this supremacy, in the actual predominance of the former over the latter.

Such is the system of Shaftesbury. The principle of our nature which distinguishes moral good and evil is a special instinct or sense, distinct from all other functions of the intelligence, whether sensation or reason; distinct also from the benevolent affections, which are the objects of its approval, and from the personal affections, which it subordinates to the benevolent affections.

Joseph Butler was born in 1692. He studied at Oxford; was preacher at the Rolls, and clerk of the closet to Queen Caroline; made Bishop of Bristol in 1738, of Durham in 1750. He died in 1752. His Fifteen Sermons were published in 1726; his Analogy in 1736. His moral system is contained chiefly in the sermons.

Without professedly adopting the theory of the moral sense, he contributed very powerfully to its development. His works contain the germes of some of the fundamental ideas afterward unfolded by Hutcheson.

Butler, like Shaftesbury, divides our instinctive affections into personal and benevolent; but he was the first who recognised that both these classes of our instinctive affections are equally disinterested: fear, hunger, etc., are no more selfish than pity, sympathy, etc.; they equally seek their respective objects directly, and without seeking anything beyond. Selfishness consists, not in the development of our personal instinctive affections, but in their being made supreme by our reflection and consent.

This distinction between the objects of our instinctive affections, and the agreeable or disagreeable feelings attending their satisfaction or disappointment, is the eminent original merit of Butler.

But, besides the instinctive affections both personal and benevolent, Butler recognises a superior principle, whose office it is to distinguish moral good and evil. This principle he calls *conscience.* In virtue of it we judge of our dispositions and affections, and feel the sentiment of obligation. Its perceptions are instinctive and immediate. Its authority is supreme. Moral good is that which conscience apprehends as such; the motive for doing it is that conscience so commands.

Butler does not precisely define the nature of conscience, and leaves it doubtful whether he considered it a sense or a rational faculty. He does not, however, explicitly declare the judgment of moral actions and the perception of obligation to be one of the functions of reason or intelligence in general; and on this account, as well as that his leading ideas have all been adopted by the sentimental moralists who followed him, he is classed among those who more expressly taught the system of the moral sense.

Francis Hutcheson was born in Ireland in 1694; studied at Glasgow; returned to Dublin, where he resided for some years as a Dissenting preacher and head of an academy; became professor of philosophy at Glasgow in 1729, where he died in 1747. His earliest work was an "Inquiry into our Ideas of Beauty and Virtue;" his last, a "System of Moral Philosophy," was published after his death by his son in 1755.

From Hutcheson the system indicated by Shaftesbury and Butler received a full development. He likewise divides our affections into personal and benevolent; those which seek our own good, and those which seek the good of others. But the point which he particularly labours in the first place to illustrate is that we desire the happiness of others directly for its own sake, so that benevolence can no more be explained by selfishness than selfishness by benevolence. Benevolence is a simple original impulse, not to be resolved into any other any more than self-love.

But, distinct from self-love and benevolence, there is a third affection of our nature, the moral sentiment. The idea of moral good is distinct both from that of our own good and from that of another's good: it cannot be explained by them; it is primitive and simple.

As the idea of moral good is simple, he concludes that the quality represented by it must be perceived by some sense, because all other simple qualities are perceived by particular senses; and that the sense must be a peculiar and distinct sense, because the quality it perceives is distinct from all others. This point, that the moral faculty is an internal sense, and not reason exercised in relation to certain objects, Hutcheson takes great pains to prove. He therefore confirms the foregoing argument by two considerations, namely, that the perception of moral goodness produces pleasure, and that it appears to us a motive of action. This pleasure is a result of the quality perceived, and therefore moral goodness cannot be resolved into the pleasure, any more than the quality of beauty can be resolved into the pleasure which accompanies the perception of it; a perception which Hutcheson also attributes to a special internal sense. The moral sense is the supreme principle.

The reality and supremacy of this principle being established, he next determines what are the dispositions of the soul in which reside the quality of moral goodness perceived by the moral sense. These are only the benevolent or disinterested affections. The personal affections which regard our own happiness may be innocent, when in subordination are so, but are not virtuous.

The moral sense, not only perceiving moral qualities, but experiencing likewise pleasure and the desires connected therewith, becomes the motive of moral action. The office of reason is reduced to that of devising means to attain the ends which our senses make known and to which our desires impel us.

Modifications of the System of Moral Sense.

There were other philosophers, who, while agreeing in the general views of the advocates of disinterested morality just expounded, that the words right and wrong express certain qualities in actions which it is the province, not of reason, but of feeling, to perceive, and that by this principle we are impelled to moral action instinctively, and therefore not by a view to our own personal pleasure or advantage, yet differed from Hutcheson and his predecessors by denying the moral sense as a special distinct faculty, and by analyzing it into other more general principles. Of these it will be sufficient to mention Hume and Adam Smith.

HUME resolves our moral ideas into a feeling of approbation or disapprobation. The moral quality of goodness, or that which excites our approbation, is utility; not merely personal, but general utility. This leaves room to consider the personal affections as good when subordinated to the benevolent affections. We approve or disapprove useful or hurtful actions by an instinct of our nature, which needs and can receive no explanation any more than our like or dislike of sweet or bitter. This constitution of our nature, by which we approve of utility in the general, is what men call *conscience;* Hume calls it *humanity.* It is quite distinct from the selfish impulse, to which it is frequently allied.

Good and evil, virtue and vice, are merely relative to our constitution. They have no objective reality no absolute and immutable character.

But the most celebrated of all the theories of disinterested morality, grounded in instinct or sentiment, is that of ADAM SMITH, contained in his Theory of the Moral Sentiments. Adam Smith was born at Kirkaldy, in Scotland, in 1723. He was educated at Glasgow and at Oxford; elected professor of logic in the University of Glasgow in 1751, of moral philosophy the year following; published his Theory of Moral Sentiments in 1759; resigned his professorship in 1763; passed the last years of his life at Edinburgh, where he died in 1790. His celebrated Wealth of Nations appeared in 1771. He was one of the most original thinkers that have ever written in the English language. He was the founder of the science of political economy; and his work on morals is no less distinguished for its originality, ingenuity, and comprehensiveness; containing such a rich collection of the most important facts, that, notwithstanding his erroneous conclusions, it is a work of the greatest value to the student of human nature. Only a brief sketch of his system can here be given.

The principle of morals is with him sympathy or fellow-feeling. This is a principle deeply implanted in human nature. It disposes us to enter into the feelings of others; it increases the strength of our feelings when shared by others; it begets in us a strong desire that our own feelings should be shared by others. This principle likewise manifests itself in, or contains the explanation of antipathies. It is governed by various laws, which are acutely described and established by Smith. So much for the principle of sympathy in general, which Smith has employed for the explanation of a vast variety of facts of human nature.

He applies this principle to the explanation of moral phenomena in the following way:

We approve the sentiments of our fellow-men when we share them or instinctively sympathize with them; we disapprove when we do not share them; and in both cases in proportion to the degree of our instinctive sympathy or antipathy. In like manner we approve or disapprove their actions, according as we do or do not sympathize with the sentiments from which they spring. The measure of moral good, or rectitude, or, as Smith terms it, *propriety*, is this instinctive sympathy. In this way we judge of the conduct of our fellow-men.

Our moral judgments of our own conduct are only applications to our sentiments and actions of judgments we have already passed with respect to our fellow-men. We thus become, in a sort, spectators of our own dispositions and actions, and instinctively sympathize with them or feel repugnant to them, as though they were the dispositions and actions of other men.—Sympathy, however, being the sole root of moral judgment, and primarily excited towards others, it followers that, if man should live alone, he would have no moral feelings or judgments.

From this twofold application of the principle of sympathy we get the most general and fundamental principle of morality: the goodness of an action is in direct proportion to the general approbation or sympathy it excites, the best actions exciting universal and unmingled sympathy.

From hence, too, the fundamental maxim of morals: act so that mankind may sympathize with you.

Experience enables us to learn the feelings awakened by sentiments and conduct; and the facts of experience generalized furnish the various particular rules of conduct which constitute practical ethics. We act from *duty* (in distinction from the immediate instinct of sympathy) when we act in conformity with these rules.

The fundamental phenomenon of moral distinctions being thus explained, the secondary phenomena are all easily explained in a corresponding way. The sentiment of *merit* and *demerit* is awakened first in relation to others; it is compounded of indirect sympathy with the person to whom the action is beneficial or injurious, and of a direct sympathy or antipathy towards the affections and motives of the agent.

Self-approbation and *remorse*, with respect to our own disposition and conduct, are explained in like manner, through our power of constructing ourselves as spectators of ourselves, and thus experiencing the pleasurable or painful sympathy excited by proper or improper dispositions.

Actions, which, by the instinctive principle of sympathy, are decided to be *proper* (right) and *meritorious*, and which by experience we are enabled to generalize under rules of conduct, are also the subject of a rational judgment of approbation in mature and cultivated minds, who are able to perceive the harmony between the instinct and the rules of experience, and also to perceive the tendency of such actions to bring the sentiments of all men into harmony, and promote the perfection of order. This order and harmony is felt to be beautiful. It is moral beauty, the source of all beauty, and produces a pleasure like that of a perfect piece of mechanism. This harmony of sentiment among men is the great end of our moral constitution.

It is a strict consequence of the system of Smith, that whatever others approve and praise will appear to us good, and what they blame will appear to us bad; and that the rule of conduct is the approbation of our fellow-men.

The instinctive desire of sympathy is the motive of all virtue, of all right conduct; a motive that sometimes operates directly, and sometimes indirectly, by the rules generalized from experience, but always to the exclusion of other motives.

Yet Smith confesses in many cases a good act will not always secure the sympathy and praise of men; that a virtuous man may sometimes have to brave the dislike of his fellows, and even the whole spirit of his age. To reconcile this with his system, he appeals to the judgment of a supposed *impartial spectator*, free from the passions and prejudices which pervert the sympathies of particular men or communities. But this impartial spectator is obviously but an *abstract spectator*, and is, in fact, nothing but the absolute and immutable judgment of that very reason or conscience which Smith repudiates, and to which he has, by his system, no right to appeal.

By a similar sophism of clandestine introduction of another principle, he endeavours to avoid the consequences of making the desire of praise the motive of virtue, by sliding from the idea of the desire of praise into that of being praiseworthy: a distinction which he cannot legitimately make, since it implies a standard not allowed in his system.

The instinctive systems of morals were animated by two different feelings: on the one hand, a dislike to the selfish system, and on the other, to the rational system. In Shaftesbury and Butler the predominant sentiment is opposition to the selfish system of Hobbes and Locke. They seem to have had no hostility to the rational system; Butler, indeed, as has been seen, leaves it doubtful whether by conscience, or the moral faculty, he meant anything more than a peculiar application of reason. Hutcheson and Hume, on the contrary, explicitly oppose the rational system. They no less distinctly deny reason to be the principle of moral ideas, than sensation in the meaning of the selfish school.

Rational Systems.

Of the rational systems, the characteristic common to them all is that of finding the origin of our moral ideas and judgments in reason. They take this ground in order to establish the absolute and immutable nature of moral distinctions both against the selfish system and against the systems of sentiment. They agree with the latter in asserting the disinterested character of moral motives; but they object against them that they make right and wrong relative to a contingent and fluctuating principle, and destroy their objective reality. Of those who held to the rational systems, some attempt to define the idea of good; others regard it as simple and undefinable. To the former class belong Wollaston and Clarke; to the latter, Price.

William Wollaston was born in 1659; educated

at Cambridge; was a teacher in Birmingham school until 1688, when, an ample fortune falling to him, he settled in London, and passed his life in studious retirement. He died in 1724. Of his writings, the best known is his Religion of Nature Delineated, in which his moral system is stated.

According to Wollaston, good is truth; and the fundamental law of action is to conform our conduct to truth.

Every action which denies a true proposition is bad. A true proposition may be denied by omission as well as by commission.

The nature of moral evil being thus determined, and good being the opposite of evil, the nature of good is likewise determined, and, consequently, the nature of actions, whether good, bad, or indifferent. A good action is one whose omission or whose opposite would be bad, that is, contradictory to the truth.

As truth and falsehood are in their nature immutable, so likewise are moral good and evil.

Such is the system of Wollaston, who thus seeks to define the idea of good. It is obvious to remark upon it: 1. That it mistakes one of the aspects or qualities of moral good for its essence: every good action does indeed contain the practical expression of a true proposition; but every true proposition, when expressed in action, does not involve the quality of moral good. 2. It confounds good and evil by its too comprehensive definition, for there is no bad action which does not contain some true propositions. 3. Many actions may imply the denial of true propositions, and therefore be absurd, while in a moral view indifferent. 4. This system is not in accordance with facts of consciousness; when we abstain from doing a wrong act, our motive is not the fear of contradicting a true proposition.

Samuel Clarke was born in 1675; educated at Cambridge, and became a clergyman of the Established Church. He published a great number of writings in theology, mathematics, metaphysics, and classical literature. He was the friend of Newton, some of whose works he translated and commented upon. He distinguished himself as a controversial writer, particularly against Leibnitz. He died in 1724.

Clarke seeks, as well as Wollaston, to define the nature of moral good. He sets out with the question concerning the motive of obligation, and brings out his idea of the nature of good in that connexion. He took this method because he was opposing the system of Hobbes, who made self-interest the foundation of duty. He examines and rejects all the forms in which the selfish theory is presented, and then propounds his own system, which is as follows: All things in the universe have their proper nature, derived from God. According to the respective natures of things arise various relations. As the essence of things is immutable, so are their relations. These relations constitute universal order. These relations are conceived by reason; they are conceived as the laws of things; and reason immediately concludes that they should be respected by rational and free beings. Hence, from the perception of relations arises the idea of obligation. When actions are conformed to these relations, they are good; when contrary, bad. Thus he arrives at the idea of the nature of good in itself, namely, order. There is an essential agreement between order and reason. Reason recognises good as order, and thereupon immediately arises the conviction of obligation. The relations of things are not the product of the mere arbitrary will of God.

This is the same system that was afterward maintained by Montesquieu. It is liable to the same general objections as that of Wollaston. It is too comprehensive; it mistakes ideas which are related to the idea of good for the essence of good: a good action is certainly conformable to the nature and relations of things; but not every action conformed to the nature of things is morally good; many are morally indifferent.

RICHARD PRICE was born in 1723. He was a Dissenting minister at Hackney. He wrote largely upon political subjects, in a democratic spirit. His moral system is contained in his Review of the Principal Questions and Difficulties in Morals. He died in 1791. As a moral philosopher, he maintained substantially the same system as that adopted by Cudworth, the principal difference being that the views of the latter received a particular form of development, as against the selfish system of Hobbes, while those of Price were expounded chiefly in opposition to the system of Hutcheson. He was a thinker of admirable penetration and sagacity, and contributed very much not only to the support of disinterested morals, but to resist the progress of the sensual system in general.

Hutcheson had taught that our ideas of good and evil are simple and original; as such, necessarily derived from a sense. From this it would follow, in strictness, that our ideas of good and evil do not designate real qualities of actions, but only the sensations which they produce in us, and therefore are as much relative to us as sweet and bitter. This conclusion Price perceived; he saw that the consequence of Hutcheson's system was not substantially different in this respect from that of the selfish system; for the selfish system makes the good and evil of an action relative merely to the pleasure or pain it produces. Hutcheson was led to his notion of a moral sense because, while, on the one hand, he wished to oppose the selfish system and to maintain disinterested morality, he yet, on the other hand, held the system of Locke, that all our simple ideas are derived from experience; he had, therefore, no way to avoid the moral consequences of Locke's system but to add to the senses recognised by Locke a *special* sense, appropriated exclusively to the perception of moral objects, which he therefore termed the *moral sense.*

In order, therefore, to establish a disinterested morality, and at the same time to establish that moral good and evil were not merely relative, but immutable and absolute, Price was led at the outset to attack the system of Locke. He therefore drew up a complete, simple, and beautiful demonstration of the insufficiency of the theory of Locke concerning the origin of ideas: a demonstration to which Reid, Stewart, and succeeding writers have added nothing original or material. He proved that there are ideas which cannot be resolved into experience, such as the ideas of cause, time, space, etc.; and as these ideas can neither be denied (as Hume attempted to do), nor resolved into experience in the sense of Locke, they must be admitted as simple primitive conceptions. If we admit them only as mere forms of the mind, as Kant afterward did, we fall into universal skepticism. We have no alternative, therefore, but to admit them as conceptions of real facts, as ideas which represent external realities, simply intelligible and not visible. These conceptions must therefore be referred to an exercise of the intelligence distinct from the empirical understanding which relates to the sensible qualities of things; they must be referred to intuitive reason, which takes cognizance of invisible relations transcending all observation and experience.

Price therefore agrees with Hutcheson in considering our ideas of good and evil as simple and primitive, and therefore derived from a faculty capable of giving them. He agrees with him in saying that we perceive good and evil in actions as we perceive extension and form in bodies. But here they part: Hutcheson concludes that these ideas can be only ideas of sensation, and therefore of a special (moral) sense, affected, as all sensibility, agreeably or disagreeably by the good or evil; Price denies this conclusion, and attributes the ideas of good and evil to a source of simple and primitive ideas overlooked by Hutcheson—intuitive reason.

Thus establishing the origin of our moral ideas in the à priori conceptions of reason, the relative and subjective character which they have in Hutcheson's system vanishes. Moral good and evil are immutable; they are what they are as necessarily and eternally as a triangle or circle is what it is. Every true moral judgment expresses absolute and eternal truth.

Price asserts the idea of good to be simple, and therefore undefinable as much as any other simple quality. In this respect he differs from the other holders of the rational system, Wollaston and Clarke. In the way of direct proof that the idea of good is undefinable, of course nothing can be adduced beyond a simple appeal to consciousness, any more than in the case of whiteness, or any other simple notion. Indirectly he attempts to prove it, by reviewing the different definitions that have been given both by rational and instinctive moralists. He shows that they are not definitions; that they are inadequate; that they all presuppose the thing to be defined; that they are dangerous.

Price recognises the fact that the contemplation of good and evil actions produces a sentiment which we express in common language by calling them pleasing or displeasing, lovely or hateful, etc. But he makes a distinction which is original and peculiar to himself. This sentiment or affection is of two kinds, partly depending upon the constitutional sensibility of each individual, and partly independent of it, absolute, and attached to reason itself.

Connected immediately with the idea of good is the idea of obligation, which springs up with it, rests upon it, and equally immutable and absolute. This rational conception of obligation is the only motive of moral action.

The conception of merit and demerit, that right doing deserves happiness, and evil doing punishment, is equally absolute, and springs up immediately upon the idea of good, and of obligation obeyed or violated. This rational conception is distinct from the fact that virtue is a source of pleasure, or that it is useful to society, and that vice is in both respects injurious: it is a necessary conception, independent of the consideration of the consequences of virtue and vice.

Reason and free-will are indispensable conditions of moral action and accountability.

Absolute virtue consists in freely and intelligently doing what is conformable to the moral law; practical virtue in doing what we believe to be conformable to it. Finite creatures are not absolutely exempt from mistake in moral any more than in other judgments. Guilt or innocence in regard to a mistake about duty are determined by the previous question whether the means of knowing were honestly used.

Sensualism in England.

But, while the advocates of a disinterested morality were led, some of them, to repudiate altogether the empirical philosophy of Locke, and others, though continuing to hold his general theory of the origin of ideas, to reject its moral conclusions, the selfish system of morals was still maintained by others, and the empiricism of Locke was carried out to a complete system of materialism and fatalism. Of the names that occur in this connexion during the period now under review—the interval, namely, between Locke and Reid—the most noticeable is that of Hartley; to which, in respect to morals, may be added that of Abraham Tucker.

DAVID HARTLEY was born in 1705; educated at Cambridge; practised medicine in Nottinghamshire and London; passed the latter part of his life at Bath, where he died in 1757. His Observations on Man were published in 1749.

This work contains a system of physiology, psychology, morals, and theology. He grounds his whole theory of the operations of the mind upon the association of ideas, and that upon the hypothesis of vibrations of the nerves in an oscillating nervous ether. These vibrations are mechanically produced by the impression of outward objects upon the nerves, propagated in the medullary substance of the nerves and brain; and a connexion between our bodies and our souls is effected through the medium of a subtile elastic ether, of which whole process the result is the state of the mind called sensations or ideas. Different ideas may become associated from being produced *contemporaneously* (which common *condition* of all the laws of association Hartley makes the sole *law*), so that one idea or vibration will propagate itself to and reproduce another, though the proper original cause of the latter, the external object, does not itself act at the time upon the nerves in reproducing its appropriate configurative vibration or idea.

With this hypothesis of vibrations mechanically set in motion, and this one and only law of association, contemporaneousness, Hartley endeavoured to explain all the phenomena of consciousness.

Ideas being with him nothing but certain determinate, configurative vibrations, it was a matter of course to find him analyzing Locke's theory of the origin of ideas into exclusive sensualism. Accordingly, he declares that "ideas of sensation are the elements of which all the others are compounded," and that he hopes to succeed in analyzing "all ideas of reflection and intellectual ideas into simple ideas of sensation;" and farther, that "*reflection is not a distinct source* [*of ideas*], as Mr. Locke makes it." Hartley thus proposed to perform for Locke's theory, by means of his principle of association, the same office that Condillac in another way attempted—to strip it, namely, of a needless and inconsistent appendage, by showing that all ideas of reflection, so called, were only sensations transformed.

Hartley was not, however, a decided materialist, although his followers at a later period pretended to simplify and perfect his theory by rejecting the notion of a thinking principle distinct from the body. Hartley allows that his theory is destructive of all the arguments "usually brought for the soul's immateriality from the subtilty of the internal senses and of the rational faculty," but at the same time acknowledges that "matter and motion," the only principles in his mechanico-physiological theory of human phenomena, "however subtly divided or reasoned upon, yield nothing but matter and motion still." He therefore desires that "he may not in any way be interpreted so as to oppose the immateriality of the soul." From this it seems that he must consent to leave the mode of the connexion between the brain and nerves and the soul, through the medium of his ether, inexplicable.

But there are other conclusions concerning the soul, repugnant to consciousness and subversive of morals, which must necessarily follow, however they might be disclaimed by him.

All the phenomena of the mind being merely sensations, or configurative vibrations mechanically produced, the soul must be a mere passive theatre, in which the products of this blind mechanism are displayed. It is destitute of all distinct faculties, of all activities, whether spontaneous or voluntary, having no power to control, determine, or modify the associations of ideas. The understanding, judgment, reason, imagination, and will, instead of actively concurring as determining or modifying causes of association, are merely its mechanical effects.

This result Hartley expressly admits in respect to the human will, denying all freedom, all self-determining power in man, and maintaining all volitions to be strictly necessary. But it is equally true of all other modes of human activity. In all human thinking, invention, and action, in science, art, and conduct, the human soul is merely the spectator of phenomena produced by an agent which itself knows nothing of what it is doing. We ourselves only fancy that we reason, love, and will. There is no intelligent activity in the universe except God, who is the grand contriver and prime mover of this mechanism.

And even the idea of God, as a rational and holy

will, is utterly inconceivable and inadmissible in Hartley's system. His theory admits of no idea of reason and free-will in man other than certain mechanical products of sensation; if these attributes be ascribed to God in this sense, we have no God properly speaking; and to suppose the mind to be in possession of different and higher ideas of these attributes as existing in God, would subvert his system.

The pious and excellent author derived, however, no such conclusions. Though he holds the necessity of human actions, and analyzes all virtue into the love of happiness, yet his second volume, in which he reasons to the common conclusions concerning God and his attributes, is almost entirely independent of the conclusions of his first. He adopts, indeed, without seeming to be aware of the inconsistency, as grounding principles, ideas which, if the doctrines of his first volume be true, can have no existence except in the vibrations of his ether.

ABRAHAM TUCKER, author of *Edward Search's Light of Nature Pursued*, 7 vols., 1768–1774, was an English gentleman of fortune, born in 1705, educated at Oxford, and died in 1774. He adopted generally the principles of Locke, which he employed chiefly in unfolding the mechanical proofs of the divine existence, and in his theory of morals. It is mainly in connexion with the latter that he is mentioned here as the author of a modification of the selfish system, which was afterward adopted and extended by Paley. Tucker cannot, indeed, be said to be the original author of it; for it is substantially the theory of Hartley, and before either of them, perhaps, of Law, bishop of Carlisle.

According to this doctrine, our moral ideas are

neither referred to reason nor to a moral sense, nor any instinctive sentiment; they are merely the result of association, and are explained in the same way as the formation of *avarice*, or any other secondary affection. Money is at first desired for the agreeable things of which it is the means; but subsequently the agreeable feelings become associated with money itself, and it comes to be desired for itself, without immediate reference to the pleasures it procures. So certain dispositions and actions, called moral, are *at first* approved or disapproved solely on account of their tendency to procure our pleasure or advantage; but in process of time we may come to associate the feelings of moral approbation and disapprobation with such dispositions and conduct, without reflecting on their tendency to procure our pleasure. In this way he contrived to elude the force of the arguments of Hutcheson and others against the fundamental principle of the selfish system, drawn from the undeniable fact of consciousness, that men do often judge and act in relation to moral objects instantaneously, and without any reference to their personal pleasure and advantage as the motive. He admits the fact, but denies that it was primitively so; and therefore maintains that all moral judgments and volitions originate at bottom in an interested personal motive.]

THE SCOTTISH SCHOOL.

REID.

THE philosophy of Hobbes and the psychology of Locke had encountered resistance more or less powerful even in England. It was felt that sensualism destroyed the principle of moral obligation, and that its true root must be sought elsewhere. Cumberland and Shaftesbury, in the seventeenth century, had placed this principle in a sentiment of benevolence and of internal satisfaction. Hutcheson, in the eighteenth century, improving the theory of benevolent affections as the source of duties, had disengaged them from any interested motive. [Other theories have also been noticed.] But this spiritualist reaction was incomplete. It supposed, or left it to be supposed [except in the work of Price], that sensualism, unable to establish moral notions, might nevertheless furnish the true basis of other orders of knowledge. Banished from the sanctuary of duty, it still reigned in the domain of speculation. But the reaction was soon generalized. Reid, who had been led by the objections of Hume to perceive the ultimate consequences of sensualism, attacked it not only as a false theory of morals, but as a false theory of the human mind.

Historical Notices.

Thomas Reid was born at Glasgow in 1710. He was at first professor of philosophy at Aberdeen, where he had pursued his studies; but in 1763 he was called by the University of Glasgow to the chair of moral philosophy, which had just before been filled by Adam Smith. His philosophical theories are contained in a treatise published under the title of *Essays on the Powers of the Human Mind,* which has been translated into French by Jouffroy. Reid had put out separately the part relative to the active and the part relative to the intellectual faculties; they were united into a single work by his disciple Dugald Stewart. After the death of his master, Dugald Stewart cultivated and enlarged the intellectual inheritance which Reid had left him. But this second representative of the Scottish school belongs, in respect to the greater part of his works, to the nineteenth century.

Exposition.

All philosophy should rest upon the observation of the operations of the human mind, and, consequently, of the faculties which produce them. The vices of the method that proceeds upon hypotheses, and the uncertainty of that which proceeds upon analogy, make us feel the necessity of this experimental basis.

The faculties of the human mind may be divided into two classes, the contemplative and the active faculties. The first relate to the understanding, the second to the will. But we must bear in mind that these powers do not work separately; the understanding intervenes in the operations of the will, and the will in the operations of the understanding.

I. *Intellectual or Contemplative Powers.*—The intellectual faculties are commonly divided into simple apprehension, judgment, and reasoning. This classification is vicious: there are operations of the mind which do not belong to either of these. For example, consciousness, which makes me aware that I am thinking, is not simple apprehension, since the latter imports neither affirmation nor negation; nor is it judgment, which is said to rest upon the comparison of two ideas; for it is not in virtue of any such comparison that we affirm our thinking. Nor is this affirmation a product of reasoning.

Renouncing the pretension of finding a strict and complete classification of the intellectual powers, Reid limits himself to enumerating those which he proposes to examine: they are: 1. The faculties which belong to our external senses; 2. Memory, 3. Conception; 4. The faculty of analyzing complex objects, and combining those that are simple; 5. Reasoning; 6. Taste; 7. Moral perception; 8. Consciousness.

In the faculties which belong to our senses, we must distinguish between the perception of external objects and the sensations which accompany it. Sensation is the feeling experienced by the mind at the presence of an external object; perception is the act by which I believe in the existence of that object.

Perception is a pure belief, independent of all demonstration, and instinctively determined by the natural constitution of the human mind.

Most philosophers have endeavoured to explain the fact of perception by saying that we do not perceive external objects themselves, but only their images present to our minds. Reid rejects this explanation: first, it is contrary to universal feeling; for all men, when they follow solely the impulse of their nature, believe they see the objects; secondly, this explanation gratuitously takes for granted the existence of images. To affirm their existence, they ground themselves upon the reason that a thing cannot act where it is not; from whence they conclude that the mind and external objects, not being in the same place, nor, consequently, immediately present to each other, there must exist an intermediate image. But Reid denies that in the fact of perception there is any action of the mind upon the object, or of the object upon the mind. For the rest, he undertakes not to substitute any explanation in the place of the one he rejects: perception is, in his view, an inexplicable fact, as the certainty of perceptions, that is, the real existence of the qualities perceived, and of the subject called matter to which they belong, is in the philosophy of Reid a belief equally necessary and obscure.

Memory implies a belief of the same nature, of which we can give no other reason than that it is an element in the constitution of our mind.

Reid describes and examines the different theories that have been proposed respecting memory, and particularly those of Locke and Hume. These theories are a consequence of the hypothesis of intermediate images, as the means by which it has been attempted to explain perception.

Conception, considered as being in general the simple apprehension of any object, material or immaterial, real or imaginary, implies in itself neither truth nor error. When we say that there are ideas, conceptions, true and false, we give to these expressions a sense which refers to an act of judgment, and not to pure conception. Reid describes the principal characteristics of conception, and particularly its analogy with the representation of an object by painting. But this analogy, true within certain limits, becomes a source of error if this comparison is transformed into an absolute similitude.

Most philosophers have maintained that conception supposes, as well as perception and memory, two objects, the one interior and immediate, the other mediate and external; in a word, the image present to the mind, and the real object which produces the image. Reid here again attacks this opinion. On this occasion he refutes, though in a very feeble way, the theory of Plato concerning ideas.

He considers, as one consequence of the distinction between the internal and the external object, the opinion according to which conception is the measure of the possibility of things. Reid makes the observation that we can conceive a proposition in two ways: first, by comprehending the signification of it; secondly, by judging that it is true. In the first case, it is false that conception is the measure of possibility, since we perfectly comprehend the meaning of a contradictory and impossible proposition; in the second case, the maxim in question is still false, since it is a matter of experience that men pass opposite judgments respecting the possibility or impossibility of things.

After simple conception comes the power of forming general conceptions. They may be considered both in relation to the words which express them, and in themselves.

And, first, how comes it that the greatest part of words are general words, while we perceive only individual existences? It should be observed, first, that there are but a very small number of individual objects perceived by the generality of men. The most part of individual objects, being visible only to the men who reside in the localities where these objects exist, have proper names; common language ought, therefore, to be in great part composed of general names. In the second place, we do not know objects in themselves, but only by their qualities or attributes, which being common to a certain number of individuals, can be expressed only by words general as themselves. Finally, this multitude of general terms results also from a want inherent in the human breast, which would be overwhelmed by the innumerable multitude of individual notions if it had not the faculty of classing them in genera and species, by means of terms which represent collections of things that have common attributes.

If we consider general conceptions in themselves, we see three processes presiding over their formation: the process of abstraction, by which a subject is resolved into its attributes, to each of which a special name is given ; the process of generalization, by which we observe the qualities common to several subjects; the process of combination, by which we unite several attributes into one single abstract whole, which is represented by a particular denomination.

The observations of Reid on the faculty of judgment contains his theory of common sense. The germe of this theory is found, as he himself has remarked, in Father Buffier's *Treatise of First Truths*, and in several other writings.

Common sense is the sound natural sense imparted to all men, in virtue of which they each and all spontaneously pass certain judgments, the evidence of which strikes all minds.

Reason has two degrees: the one consists in judging of things evident in themselves, the other in deducing from those judgments consequences which were not evident in themselves. The first is the peculiar and the only function of common sense; from which it appears that common sense coincides in its whole extent with reason, and is only one of its degrees.

This laid down, it is necessary to determine the judgments which are the product of common sense. These judgments should first be divided into two classes, according as they refer to contingent truths or to necessary truths.

The judgments of common sense relating to contingent truths are, according to Reid, the following principles:

1. Everything which is attested to me by consciousness and the internal sense really exists.

2. The thoughts of which I am conscious are thoughts of a being whom I call *I*.

3. The things which memory distinctly recalls to me really happened.

4. I am certain of my personal identity from the remotest period to which my memory can reach.

5. Objects which I perceive by the aid of my senses really exist, and are as I perceive them.

6. I exert some degree of power upon my actions and determinations.

7. The natural faculties by which I distinguish truth from error are not delusive.

8. My fellow-men are living and intelligent creatures like myself.

9. Certain expressions of countenance, certain sounds of the voice, and certain gestures, indicate certain thoughts and certain dispositions of mind.

10. We have naturally some regard for the testimony of men in matters of fact, and even for human authority in matters of opinion.

11. Many events which depend upon the free-will of our fellow-men may nevertheless be foreseen with more or less probability.

12. In the order of nature, that which is to take place will probably resemble that which has taken place in similar circumstances.

With respect to the judgments of common sense which relate to necessary truths, Reid limits himself to dividing them into classes, indicating some examples, to which he adds observations on such of these principles as have been the subject of controversies. These judgments of common sense are grammatical, logical, mathematical, esthetical, moral, and metaphysical. Among the metaphysical principles he distinguishes three which have been attacked by Hume, namely, that sensible qualities have a subject which we call body, and a subject which we call spirit; that everything which begins to exist is produced by a cause; and that evident marks of design and intelligence in the effect prove design and intelligence in the cause. Hume had maintained that these principles, if true, must have their foundation in experience; and yet, nevertheless, experience teaches us nothing concerning their truth. Reid replied that it is not necessary to put their basis where Hume sought it; that it is found in the natural belief, which he designates by the term common sense.

Reid then treats of the faculty of reasoning and of its general characteristics. In this connexion he inquires whether morals is susceptible of demonstration; that is, whether the first principles of morals can be deduced from principles logically anterior: a question which he resolves in the negative. Moral axioms are perceived intuitively, and are an immediate product of common sense.

Taste, which is an intellectual faculty, analogous in certain respects to the physical sense by which we perceive savours, has three principal objects, novelty, grandeur, beauty. The reason of the pleasure we experience from novelty is found in the very constitution of man, who, by nature active, feels the want of developing himself. Grandeur pleases because it is a manifestation of power, naturally preferable to weakness. The sentiment of the beautiful is composed of two elements, of an agreeable emotion, and of the belief that there exists a real perfection in the objects which produce the emotion.

Consciousness is the faculty that makes us aware of the actual modifications and operations of our own minds. Skeptics have assailed all other orders of knowledge, but have never disputed the facts of consciousness. But it will not do to confound consciousness with reflection. The first, which results necessarily from the very nature of man, is common to all; the second requires a capacity of intellectual activity which is given but to a few, and this is the reason there are so many disputes concerning the constitution and faculties of the human mind, although we have immediate knowledge of them. It is because it does not proceed upon consciousness alone, but depends in a great part upon reflection.

As to moral perception, which is a faculty at once intellectual and active, Reid refers the questions relating to it to his observation on the second class of human faculties.

II. *Active Faculties.*—These suppose the ideas of active power. That we have in ourselves such a power is proved by universal language, which implies the distinction of active and passive, and by the practical life of all men. This idea, it is true, is furnished neither by sensations nor by consciousness, which testifies solely the existence of the operations, and not the existence of the faculties. But, since this idea is inherent in the human mind, we must look for its source in a belief resulting from the constitution of the human mind.

Although the will be that which we can conceive most clearly under the notion of active power, we ought nevertheless to distinguish the principles of action into two classes, mechanical principles and voluntary principles. The mechanical principles, which suppose neither attention, nor deliberation, nor will to act, are the instincts and habits. Besides the instincts which are manifested in the child, there are some which survive infancy. Some are absolutely necessary to our physical preservation, such as the instinct which governs the act of swallowing. Others refer to actions which must be so frequently repeated that they would absorb our whole attention if they required any deliberation. Others, again, refer to actions which must be produced so suddenly that thought would not have time to intervene. We may attribute, at least partially, to instinct the natural propensity of man for imitation. As to habits, they suppose undoubtedly the action of the will, in the sense that they consist in a facility of action acquired by repeated acts; but the proper power of habit, taken in itself, has its root in a property of human nature distinct from simple will.

The principles of voluntary actions are of two sorts, for the will or power of self-determination is influenced by two sorts of motives: irrational motives, relating to the faculty of feeling, and rational motives, relating to the faculty of judging. The first, common to man and the brutes, are addressed to the animal part of our nature; the second correspond to the human element properly speaking.

The animal principles of action are resolved into appetites, desires, and affections. The appetites are periodical, and accompanied by a disagreeable sensation peculiar to each. The desires are not accompanied by a disagreeable sensation; nor are they periodical, but constant. The affections are principles of action which imply a benevolent or malevolent disposition with respect to persons. When the desires and affections are carried to a certain degree of vehemence, they take the name of passions.

The rational principles, or those relative to the faculty of judging, are enlightened self-love and duty. Enlightened self-love, taken as the sole regulative principle of human conduct, is insufficient. The generality of men do not possess sufficient instruction to be able to make a skilful application of it at all times. It does not elevate man to the perfection of which humanity is susceptible; for disinterestedness and generosity are the most elevated objects of our sympathy and admiration. And, finally, it cannot by itself procure the greatest amount of happiness, since men who consult only their own welfare, however strictly their conduct may coincide in form with our notions of perfect virtue, are deprived of the high internal satisfaction connected only with the fulfilment of duty.

The notion of duty, which is found naturally in the minds of all men, testifies the existence of a [moral faculty, which Reid does not object to calling, with Hutcheson], *moral sense*, which inspires us with primitive moral judgments, as the senses inspire us with the primitive judgments we pass respecting bodies. But there is this difference between speculative and moral judgments, that the latter are accompanied by a sentiment of approbation or disapprobation, while the former are pure affirmations separate from any emotion.

The moral sense, or conscience, has need, like all human faculties, to be cultivated in order to develop and perfect it.

Summarily, enlightened self-interest is a rational principle, regulative of all the animal principles which refer to utility, and ought itself to be regulated by the rational principle of duty. But can it ever happen that these two principles should be really in opposition? Faith in divine Providence should persuade us that we can never injure our own welfare by taking duty for our guide. Take away the belief in God, and these two constituent principles of our actions might come, and would necessarily come, into a state of hostility; and this is a proof that morals is necessarily connected with religion.

But, whatever be the motives that excite it, the will is free. Wherever there is passivity, there is, properly speaking, no cause: to affirm that man is free is to affirm that he is really the cause of his own actions. In developing the proofs of human freedom, and in replying to the principal objections alleged against it, Reid employs the grounding ideas found in anterior philosophies. The enumeration which he gives of first principles in morals, and the considerations which he offers upon the conditions of morality, on the character of the idea of justice, which is natural and not artificial, and upon the nature of the obligation of contracts, present also a class of ideas not pertaining to the Scottish philoso phy in its fundamental peculiarities.

Observations.

1. In respect of method, the philosophy of Reid was a combination of the method of Descartes and that of Bacon. Descartes set out with internal observation, but he soon abandoned it. Bacon, on his part, had established that philosophy should rest upon a large basis of observation; but he had particularly applied his method to the knowledge of external facts. Reid, uniting these two points of view, took, as the basis of philosophy, the most complete observation possible of internal facts, or of the constitution of the human mind.

2. Whatever judgment be passed upon the general principles of his philosophy, it must be allowed to contain a multitude of views which evince remarkable sagacity.

3. That which specially characterizes his philosophy is his doctrine concerning ultimate conviction, or the judgments of common sense. The Scottish school has well perceived that the human mind implies radically, and under many relations, an element of belief independent of all demonstration, and that every philosophy which rejects this element undermines the edifice it would construct. But, while most other philosophies require speculative concep-

tions where only the fact of belief is to be had, does not the Scottish school take refuge too often in the convenient asylum of belief, in order to excuse itself from furnishing speculative grounds?

4. Many modern metaphysicians, particularly in Germany, abandoning themselves to a philosophical intemperance, which misconceives the limits of the human mind, have resembled a man who intoxicates himself under the pretext that it is necessary to drink. The Scottish school almost refuses to drink for fear of intoxication. Its tendency to error is that of an excess of circumspection, and that of other schools is that of an excess of boldness. But by its firm and practical good sense it has served as a most important counterpoise to the license of speculation.

APPENDIX.

SKETCH OF THE HISTORY OF PHILOSOPHY FROM REID TO THE PRESENT TIME.

APPENDIX.

ENGLISH PHILOSOPHY IN THE CLOSE OF THE EIGHTEENTH CENTURY.

FROM the time of Reid to the end of the eighteenth century, a considerable degree of philosophical activity prevailed in England and Scotland, and numerous works were produced, though in general the religious and moral predominated over the purely speculative interest. The philosophical writings of the period for the most part belong, in respect to their leading principles, to the school of Locke and Hartley, or to the Scottish school represented by Reid. A brief notice will be given of some of the more distinguished names, and of the position in which they respectively stand in relation to anterior systems.

Opponents of Hume.

OSWALD.—BEATTIE.—PRIESTLEY.

THE skepticism which Hume had deduced from the principles of Locke, assailing, as it did, not only the pretensions of speculation, but the certainty of all human knowledge, and especially the fundamental truths of religion, the existence of God, Providence, a future life, miracles, etc., called out many adversaries, who in various ways sought to defend the truths of religion against the conclusions of Hume.

JAMES OSWALD, a clergyman of the Established Church of Scotland, published in 1766–1772 an *Ap-*

peal to Common Sense in Behalf of Religion, in which he made the Common Sense of mankind, or the universal consent of humanity, the first principle and supreme criterion of all philosophical truth.

James Beattie (born in 1735, died in 1803), professor of Moral Philosophy at Edinburgh, and afterward at Aberdeen, produced in 1770 his *Essay on the Nature and Immutability of Truth.* He adopted the same general system as Reid, recognising certain principles of knowledge as not derived from experience in the meaning of Locke and Hume, but referable to Common Sense: he used these terms, however, in a very vague and exceptionable way. He defended the truths attacked by skepticism with great zeal, but with far less ability than Reid. He published also various treatises on Æsthetics and Morals, in which last he maintained the system of the moral sense. As a writer, he is more remarkable for elegance and good taste than for philosophical genius.

Joseph Priestley, who was born in 1733 and died in 1804, is more celebrated at the present day for his contributions to physical science than for his philosophical writings. He attacked, however, both Hume and his adversaries. Priestley was a materialist, and an ardent disciple of Hartley, whose theory of association he adopted and revived, as explaining all the phenomena of the human mind. Accordingly, while he attempted to refute the objections of Hume against the truths of natural and revealed religion, he at the same time combated the doctrines of Reid, Beattie, and Oswald concerning Common Sense, or instinctive principles of belief not resolvable into sensation. These principles he ridiculed as *occult qualities,* which should be exploded from philosophy. With Hartley, he likewise denied the freedom of the will, and maintained the necessity of all human volitions.

Ethical Systems.

FERGUSON.

NEARLY at the same time with the first publication of Reid appeared the "Institutes of Moral Philosophy" by Adam Ferguson. Ferguson was born in 1724, was professor of Moral Philosophy in the University of Edinburgh, which place he resigned in 1783 in favour of Dugald Stewart. His "Treatise on Moral and Political Science" was published in 1793. He died in 1816. He maintained the doctrine of the moral sense, and made virtue to consist in a continuous effort, by which the perfection of the soul is developed.

PALEY.

WILLIAM PALEY (born in 1743 and died in 1805) published his celebrated work on Moral Philosophy in 1785. He agrees with Hume in resolving the essence of virtue into utility, yet he differs from him, as well as from the other advocates of disinterested morality, by denying the existence of conscience, of any moral faculty, considered either as a moral sense, or as a modification of reason. Paley was a strenuous supporter of the selfish system, though not in its grossest form. The general consequences of actions is the sole criterion of their moral quality. Virtue is defined by him to be "the doing good to mankind, in obedience to the will of God, for the sake of everlasting happiness." Mackintosh makes the observation that this is not so much a definition as a proposition. Taken, however, as a definition, it involves the gravest consequences: among others, that an act even of obedience to the will of God (which, unless his definition involve a contradiction, must be taken only as the rule of action) is destitute of the character of virtue if a regard to our own happiness was not the motive. Conformably with his principles, he makes no distinction between Prudence and Virtue, except that the former relates to our regard to what we shall gain or lose in this world, the latter to what we shall gain or lose in the world to come; that is to say, he makes no essential distinction between them.

DARWIN.

ERASMUS DARWIN was born in 1732 and died in 1802. Besides several poetical works, he wrote numerous treatises on different subjects of physical and physiological science. His philosophical views are particularly developed in his Zoonomia, or Laws of Organic Life, published in 1793–1796. He belonged in general to the school of Hartley and Priestley, though he developed his views with much originality. He taught that all animated nature originates in single filaments, endowed with irritability, which is the cause of vital motion and organization. He carried his materialism to such an exaggerated extreme as to maintain that "ideas are material things:" a position which he does not even attempt to prove, but reasons upon throughout his work as an established fact. It is worthy of notice, that the English physiological materialists of this period carried their views on this subject to a much greater length, and expressed them much more decidedly, than the French followers of Locke; for, while the latter held merely in a general way that thought is the *result* of material organization, and that "every idea must," in the language of Diderot, "necessarily resolve itself ultimately into a sensible representation or picture," several of the former advanced the special hypothesis that the immediate objects of thought are either particles of the medullary substance of the brain, or vibrations of these particles. The doctrine of the materiality of ideas cannot be said to be original with Darwin: it appeared in the seventeenth century in the writings of Sir Kenelm Digby, and also of Dr. Robert Hooke, celebrated for his attempts to deprive Newton of the honour of his discoveries with respect to the law of gravitation. One of the early works of Dr. Thomas Brown was devoted to the needless labour of refuting Darwin's theory.

BENTHAM.

Among the modern advocates of the selfish system of morals, no one has attracted a greater share of public attention than Jeremy Bentham. This celebrated jurist was born in 1747; was educated at Oxford; was called to the bar, but soon abandoned the profession, and led a retired and singular mode of life in the heart of London, devoting himself to the composition of numerous works on jurisprudence, government, and various branches of political and moral science. He died in 1832. The eccentricity of his character and habits; the peculiarities of his style; the decided and exclusive cast of his principles; the hardihood with which he carried them out to their consequences; the uncompromising hostility with which he assailed all opinions differing from his own; and the seemingly practical character of his system: these circumstances have conspired to make him the head of an ardent school of disciples, who have continued to the present time to propagate the doctrines of their master with a zeal almost bordering upon fanaticism. As a jurist, he has certainly rendered important service to humanity, and shed much original light upon many principles of legislation, in spite of the errors into which the unqualified and exclusive character of his principles led him. As a moralist, his system is substantially that of Hobbes, his originality consisting only in the boldness of his positions, and in the peculiar form in which he has clothed them. Hobbes was a metaphysician, Bentham a jurist: Hobbes sought to ground his principles in psychological analysis; Bentham assumed them without proof as obvious and undeniable facts. As a jurist, Bentham was led to regard human actions in the single point of their influence upon society; for, though legislation does not, and ought not to, disregard the moral quality of actions, yet its peculiar and immediate object is the prevention of actions injurious to society. Thus Bentham, setting out as a jurist, becomes a moralist only by extending the maxims of legislative enactment to all human actions, and making their private and social utility the sole test of their morality. His moral system is mainly found in his *Principles of Morals and Legislation*, published in 1789, though it had been printed nine years before.

The principles of his system are briefly as follows:

The desire of pleasure and the fear of pain are the only possible motives which can influence the human will.

Consequently, pleasure is the only object of pursuit, the sole end of human existence.

The *utility* of actions is their property of increasing the sum of happiness, or lessening the amount of suffering, in individuals or in the community.

The *lawfulness, justice, goodness*, or *morality* of actions means only their utility in the sense defined:

if these terms are not used in this sense, they are used without meaning.

The *principle of utility*, or the *greatest happiness principle*, is that which determines the quality of actions by their twofold property of producing pleasure or pain in the individual or the community. This is the only test of the morality of actions, the sole ground of approbation or disapprobation, the sole rule for morals as well as legislation.

The supreme interest of every individual is the attainment of the greatest happiness of which he is capable; the supreme interest of society is the attainment of the greatest happiness possible to all the individuals of which it is composed.

All systems of ethics and of legislation which proceed upon any other principle than utility are false: all false systems may be reduced to two classes: 1. Systems of *asceticism*, which adopt, indeed, the right criterion by judging of the quality of actions from their consequences, but apply it falsely and in contradiction to human nature by making good actions to be such as produce pain, and bad actions such as produce pleasure; 2. Systems of *sympathy and antipathy*, which judge of actions as good or bad independently of their consequences.

The principle of utility being thus assumed as absolute, it follows that every kind of pleasure—even that felt by the perpetrator of the most atrocious crime—is good in itself; the man is not to be condemned for the pleasure he took in the act, but only because its ulterior consequences will produce an overbalance of pain: this is the only reason why it is called wrong or criminal.

It is in the practical application of these principles, and especially in his character of jurist, that the originality of Bentham is displayed. Having classified the various kinds of pleasure and pain, he seeks to determine their comparative value, and thus to fix a graduated scale for the moral valuation of human actions. To make this calculation, it is necessary to have the elements to be compared. These are referred to four classes: 1. All the pleasures and pains of which human nature is susceptible, compared in the sixfold relation of *intensity, duration, certainty* or *uncertainty, propinquity* or *remoteness, fecundity,* and *purity;* 2. Primary circumstances, tending to increase or lessen the value of those pleasures, as health, strength, etc.; 3. Secondary circumstances, affecting the degree of sensibility, and indirectly modifying the value of the pleasures and pains of individuals; 4. The multiplied consequences which follow a pleasurable or painful action, beginning with the individual, and extending through the various domestic and social relations to the community at large.

Applying these elements of calculation, all practical problems in morals are solved, and the moral value of every possible act is determined. If an action is useful, it is good; if injurious, bad; and in both cases in the degree of its utility or injuriousness: and to decide in every particular case, we must calculate all its possible effects to see which preponderates, the pleasurable or the painful consequences. To know which of two useful or of two injurious actions is the most so, the same rule applies. The relative goodness or badness of a given number of good or bad actions is determined in the same way.

But the main value of this method, in the view of Bentham, is in its application to the grounds of legislation. To inquire whether mankind have the right to regard and punish certain actions as crimes, is the same thing as to inquire whether doing so is useful to society. But the crime (the injurious action) is an evil, and the penalty is an evil. The question, therefore, is to be decided by a balance struck between two evils: Will the penalty tend to prevent the crime; and is the evil of the penalty less than that of the consequences of the act? If so, we may forbid and punish. That it is so in certain cases is easily proved; therefore society has in certain cases the right to forbid and punish.

As pleasure and pain are the only motives that can determine the will, they are the only *sanctions* which can operate with binding or obligatory force. There are four kinds of sanctions: *physical*, referring to the natural consequences of actions; *moral* or *popular*, referring to the pleasures and pains resulting from the opinions and feelings excited towards us by our actions in the minds of our fellow-men; the *religious*, which result from the hope and fear of rewards and punishments in a future life; and, lastly, the *political* sanction, including the penalties attached to actions by law.

Of these sanctions civil society, or government, can directly use only the last. It can prohibit certain actions, and punish them with certain pains; but it cannot control the physical or moral consequences of actions. It should not, however, disregard the other sanctions; on the contrary, it should render them as far as possible auxiliary to the influence of the legal sanction.

Observations.

The whole system of Bentham rests upon the position that pleasure and pain are the sole motives of human volition. Bentham assumes this principle as an axiom that needs no proof, and he offers none, except indirectly, in combating the systems that admit another motive.

The plausibility of many of his explanations of human conduct is entirely owing, however, to a confusion which he has made of two principles perfectly distinct: the principle of private utility, and the principle of general utility. Bentham made this confusion quite unconsciously; Hobbes was more clear-sighted and more consistent: he saw the distinction, and refused to make the substitution. To lay down, first, our own personal pleasure, advantage, or interest, as the sole and absolute rule of action, and then to lay down the pleasure, advantage, or interest of society, as if it were the same thing, is to confound two rules altogether distinct and different. Bentham did not perceive the confusion, because he did not perceive the distinction between the two rules. His mode of arguing, in respect to the reasons which lead us to regulate our conduct in accordance with the general welfare of society, shows that he makes a view to our personal advantage the motive even for obeying the rule of general utility. This is consistent with his system; for his fundamental principle legitimately gives but one rule of action, regard to our private interest; any other rule is inconsistent: a regard to public utility can be a legitimate motive only as a means to a private end; that is to say, is not a motive at all. Yet, although his fundamental principle gives but this one motive, and although his own analysis resolves a regard for public utility into a mere regard for private and personal advantage as the ultimate and sole motive, he nevertheless, in other passages, reasons in a way which is correct only upon the ground that a regard for general utility is a rule and motive of itself; and it is to this inconsistency that his system owes much of its plausibility, its seeming accordance with the facts of human nature. A regard to our own interest is undoubtedly *one* of the motives of human volition: the error of Bentham, as of every selfish system, consists in making it the *sole* motive.

PHILOSOPHY IN THE NINETEENTH CENTURY.

Since the commencement of the present century, England, Germany, and France have continued to be, as they were in the preceding century, the principal centres of philosophical activity. No original or important systematic work has appeared, and but few contributions to speculative science have been made in any other country. Philosophy has been cultivated in England, however, much less generally, and with much less interest, than in Germany and France.

ENGLISH PHILOSOPHY IN THE NINETEENTH CENTURY.

STEWART.

Dugald Stewart was born at Edinburgh in 1753, and was educated in the University of that city, though he afterward attended the lectures of Reid at Glasgow. In 1785 he succeeded his father in the mathematical professorship in the University of Edinburgh, which he subsequently exchanged for the chair of Moral Philosophy, vacated by the resignation of Ferguson. He published the first volume of his Philosophy of the Human Mind in 1798; the remainder of his writings belong to the nineteenth century. He died in 1828.

Stewart was the disciple of Reid, whose general system he adopted. A regular analysis of the leading principles contained in his writings is, therefore, unnecessary in this place; and even the modifications which he introduced into the system of his master are for the most part so cautiously suggested, and so generally connected with its subordinate principles or with its particular applications, that a detailed enumeration of them does not fall within the compass of this sketch. The general character of his labours should, however, be noticed: they occupy a distinct and important place in the history of modern philosophy, on account of the important influence they exerted in diffusing a taste for philosophical studies, in spreading the principles of Reid, and in opposing the progress of sensualism, particularly in its relations to morals.

Stewart was superior to Reid in elegance of taste, and in variety and extent of philosophical learning. To this, in connexion with the critical cast of his mind, and his modest and cautious disposition, it was owing, more, perhaps, than to the want of original power, that his works are mainly occupied with critical disquisitions attached to the principles of Reid, and present so little attempt at systematic peculiarities of his own. It is by no means true, however, that he contributed nothing to philosophy but critical disquisitions and tasteful illustrations of the principles of his master. It has been said of him that he took more pains to conceal his originality than most men take to display their own. That he was not deficient in talent for original observation and in speculative ability, might be shown from various parts of his writings; as, for instance, his remarks on casual associations; on dreaming; on causation; and on the difference between man and the lower animals.

He adopted the method of Reid, and he followed him in his controversy against the too narrow and exclusive principles of Locke; but on both these important subjects he has shed much light, particularly upon the latter, by his critical ability, and by his talent for illustration.

He accepted Reid's classification of the faculties of the human mind; but he has enlarged and completed his system by a fuller and more perfect analysis of many important faculties. In the second volume of his Elements of the Philosophy of the Mind, by his discussions concerning the process of reasoning and the principles of evidence, he has contributed very valuable materials to logic, of the importance of which, as comprehending far more than the artificial systems of deduction, he had a very strong impression.

Among the instances in which he has departed from the views of Reid, may be mentioned his doctrines concerning association of ideas and habit. Reid denied that the association of ideas has its ground in an ultimate principle or fact of our mental constitution, and resolved it into habit, which he regarded as an original principle. Stewart, on the other hand, resolves habit into association. But one of the most important modifications which Stewart has effected in the philosophy of Reid, consists in substituting the terms Fundamental Laws of Human Thought or Belief in place of Reid's principles of Common Sense. This change is made in his characteristic modest and cautious way. He vindicates Reid from the charge of holding this term in the vague and unphilosophical sense of Beattie, but none the less clearly does he see and expose the inconveniences and objectionable consequences of retaining such a term at all, as referring to the absolute and necessary convictions of pure reason.

In morals, Stewart has filled up many chasms left in Reid's works by his more systematic and complete analysis of the various practical principles of human nature. Equally with Reid, he was the earnest opponent of every form of the selfish system; with still more clearness than his master, though in his usual guarded and cautious tone, he distinguishes his system from the instinctive or sentimental systems. He has contributed much to set in a strong light the essential and immutable difference of right and wrong, and the absolute authority of conscience as a conviction of obligation, grounded necessarily and immediately upon the perception of right and wrong. In regard to the term moral sense, which the influence of Hutcheson had brought into general use, and which Reid adopted, though Stewart does not repudiate it, yet he clearly shows, in his remarks on the objections to the objective reality and immutability of moral distinctions which may be drawn from the term, that he does not hold to the moral sense as a *special faculty* of perceiving moral ideas. "The words *cause and effect*, *duration*, *identity*, and many others, express simple ideas, as well as the words *right* and *wrong;* and yet it would surely be absurd to ascribe each of them to a particular power of perception." From this it clearly appears that he takes the moral sense simply as a form of the reason, and that he regards the latter as the faculty in which our moral conceptions originate. In this view he expressly vindicates the use of the word by Cudworth and Price; with whose doctrines on this subject, as well as with that of Kant, his own is identical. With respect to the last named philosopher, it may be remarked, that Stewart indulged himself in a prejudice which a better acquaintance with his principles would have materially modified. The strange and uncouth terminology of the German was likely to be peculiarly repulsive to a taste like Stewart's; yet, in spite of their differences in this respect, and in spite of still more important differences in doctrine, the coincidence between their opinions, and the substance of their reasoning on many material points, is remarkable enough to have been the subject of frequent observation.

BROWN.

THOMAS BROWN was born in 1777, and educated at the University of Edinburgh. At the age of twenty he wrote a refutation of Darwin's Zoonomia, which at once distinguished him as a person of superior ability. In 1810 he succeeded Stewart as professor of Moral Philosophy at Edinburgh. He was the author of several poetical works, the principal of which is the Paradise of Coquettes, and displays considerable poetical talent. He also published an Inquiry into the Relation of Cause and Effect. His lectures on the Philosophy of the Human Mind were published after his death. He was cut off by consumption in 1820.

Brown classes the subjects which fall within the scope of the Philosophy of the Human Mind under four general divisions: the Physiology of the Mind; Ethics, Politics, and Natural Theology. He makes the first the principal object of his inquiries. The following analysis exhibits the leading principles and main doctrines of his system:

Psychology is with him a physiology or physical study of the mind, considered as a substance susceptible of various states of feeling. These various states of feeling are the phenomena of the mind, and are only the one mind itself existing in different modifications.

It is the object of philosophy to observe and generalize these phenomena until we arrive at general laws, which laws are nothing but the most general expression of the circumstances in which the phenomena are felt to agree.

The principles of the investigation of the phenomena of the mind are precisely the same as in the investigation of matter or external nature, the only difference being in the circumstance that in the physics of matter the object of inquiry and the inquiring subject are different, while in the physics of the mind they are the same.

This leads to a discussion of the principles of physical inquiry in general, as applicable to mind no less than to matter.

All inquiry with respect to the various substances in nature must regard them either as they exist in *space* or as they exist in *time:* we inquire either into their *composition* or into their *changes.* A substance, considered as it exists in space, is the mere name which we give to bodies, similar or dissimilar, in apparent continuity; as it exists in time, it is that which is the subject or the antecedent of changes, and we inquire into its susceptibilities and into its powers.

But here we note the intervention of a principle different from the mere present perception of particular phenomena in succession. Our senses, our experience, show us only what *is,* not what *has been* nor what *will be.* Yet the observation of any changes, any phenomena in succession, is accompanied with the irresistible belief that in the same circumstances the like changes have invariably taken place and will invariably take place, or, in other words, that the same antecedents will invariably be followed by the same consequents.

As this belief cannot be derived from experience, so neither can it be resolved into custom, as has been attempted by Hume. It is an *instinctive* belief, a feeling which on certain occasions arises in virtue of the original constitution of the mind, just as our simple sensations or emotions arise on their proper occasions.

As to the nature of the relation to which this belief attaches, it is merely one of invariable antecedence and consequence. The term Power signifies nothing more than the antecedence of phenomena to other phenomena in an invariable order; Cause signifies nothing but the invariable antecedent; and Effect nothing but the invariable consequent in a given sequence of phenomena. If we use these words to signify anything more, we use them without meaning. There is no such thing as power or cause other than as a mere invariable antecedent; and no such thing as effect other than as a mere invariable consequent. The antecedent and the cause are not distinct, though inseparable; they are identical: so likewise of the consequent and the effect. In any invariable sequence of phenomena, as the explosion of powder following the contact of fire; or the motion of the arm following a particular state of the mind; or the creation of the world following the will of God: if we suppose there is any *bond* of connexion between the phenomena; anything except the mere fact of the succession itself; any *ground* of the succession which lies under it in the substances of the phenomena; any power, cause, or efficacy which determines the invariable antecedence and consequence, and makes it a necessary connexion, we delude ourselves with mere words without significance.

The philosophy of matter and the philosophy of mind agree in this respect, that our knowledge of both is confined to the mere phenomena. They agree also in the two species of inquiry they admit: the phenomena of mind, like those of matter, may be considered as *complex,* and susceptible of analysis, or they may be considered as *successive* in a certain *order,* and bearing, therefore, the reciprocal relations of cause and effect. The phenomena of the mind are, however, only relatively complex, and analysis is only the virtual decomposition of a seeming complexity. Analysis, in the science of the mind, is founded wholly upon the feeling of relation which one state of mind seems to us to bear to other states of mind as comprehensive of them. It is chiefly, if not wholly, as an analytical science that philosophy can be a science of progressive discovery.—So much for the nature, objects, and method of the physiology of the mind.

Before proceeding to the classification and particular analysis of the various states of the mind, it is necessary to consider two general facts always implied in the variety of phenomena: these facts are comprehended in the terms *consciousness* and *personal identity.*

Consciousness is neither any special separate faculty of the mind, having the office of rendering us aware of the various feelings of the mind, as Doctor Reid makes it to be, nor, on the other hand, is it a fact or state of the mind distinct from the feelings themselves of which we are aware, and the condition of our being aware of them: it is merely a general term expressive of the collective whole of our various states of mind. There are not sensations, thoughts, passions, AND also consciousness, any more than there is a quadruped apart from the particular animals included under the term. To be conscious of particular feelings, be they sensations, thoughts, or volitions, is nothing but to feel in a particular way, is nothing but to have the sensation, thought, or volition. When we use the term as if it implied more than this—as if the sensation, etc., were one thing, and the consciousness of it another thing—we express nothing but the remembrance of former feelings, and a feeling of the relation of our different feelings to a permanent subject.

This notion of the mind as the permanent subject of the all various feelings that come and go within us, is expressed in the words self, or personal identity. Consciousness and memory are the conditions of the notion and belief of self, or personal identity. In memory it is not merely a past feeling that arises to us, but a feeling recognised to have been formerly felt by us as the same beings who now remember it. Brown makes no distinction between the notion of *self*, merely as the *subject* of a feeling distinct from the feeling, and the notion of *identity*, as implying the unchanged *sameness* of the subject amid the changing of its feelings; and hence makes memory the condition of the notion, denying the view of Stewart that every exercise of consciousness, without reference to the past, implies the notion of self.

Brown agrees with Stewart in referring the origin of the idea and belief of self and personal identity to a law of thought, or intuitive principle grounded in the constitution of the mind. He gives for characteristics of an intuitive principle, that the conception or belief which it expresses is universal, immediate, and irresistible; and vindicates the validity of such principles as the ground of belief.

After these general views, the next thing is the more particular analysis and classification of the various phenomena of the mind. Dissatisfied with all previous classifications, and with the grounds upon which they have proceeded, Brown produce one sentirely new, both in its nomenclature and in the distinctions which are taken as the basis of the arrangement. All the phenomena of the mind are here arranged under two divisions, External Affections of the Mind, or those which arise immediately in consequence of external things, and Internal Affections, which arise in consequence of previous affections of the mind itself.

The following table exhibits the classification of the phenomena under this primary division :

DIVISION I.

EXTERNAL AFFECTIONS OF THE MIND.

ORDER I.

THE LESS DEFINITE EXTERNAL AFFECTIONS.

CLASS I.

Appetites; as Hunger, etc

CLASS II.

Muscular Pains.

CLASS III.

Muscular Pleasures.

ORDER II.

THE MORE DEFINITE EXTERNAL AFFECTIONS.

CLASS I.

Sensations of Smell.

CLASS II.

Sensations of Taste.

CLASS III.

Sensations of Hearing.

CLASS IV.

Sensations of Touch.

CLASS V.

Sensations of Sight.

DIVISION II.

THE INTERNAL AFFECTIONS OF THE MIND.

ORDER I.

INTELLECTUAL STATES OF THE MIND.

CLASS I.

Simple Suggestions · Suggestions of Resemblance, Contrast, Contiguity.

CLASS II.

Relative Suggestions, or Feelings of Relation.

SPECIES I.

Relations of Coexistence, Position, Resemblance, Degree, Proportion, Comprehensiveness.

SPECIES II.

Relations of Succession.

ORDER II.

EMOTIONS; SUCH AS LOVE, ETC.

CLASS I.

Immediate Emotions.

SPECIES I.

Immediate Emotions involving no Moral Feeling:

Cheerfulness & Melancholy;
Wonder;
Languor;
Beauty and its Opposite;
Sublimity;
The Ludicrous.

SPECIES II.

Immediate emotions involving some Moral Feeling:

Feelings distinctive of Virtue and Vice:
Love and Hate;
Sympathy;
Pride and Humility.

CLASS II.

Retrospective Emotions.

SPECIES I.

Retrospective Emotions, having reference to others:

Anger;
Gratitude.

SPECIES II.

Retrospective Emotions, having reference to ourselves:

Simple Regret and Gladness;
Remorse and its Opposite.

CLASS III.

Prospective Emotions, comprehending our Desires & Fears.

In treating of the sensations which are ascribed to touch, Brown denies the common distinction of the qualities of matter into primary and secondary, contending that both alike express merely states of the sentient mind, which by the constitution of our nature we are irresistibly led to attribute to external causes. He therefore denies that there is any special faculty called *Perception* distinct from the sensation. There is the state of mind consequent upon the presence of an object to the sense of touch, and this state of mind, this sensation, or feeling of resistance, is all there is in the process of perception, except the intuitive belief in an external cause suggested by the associating principle.

Reid held the intuitive knowledge both of mind and of matter, and regarded the reality of their antithesis, whether it could be explained or not, as a fundamental unquestionable truth.

Brown held consciousness in perception to be a mere modification (state of feeling) of the percipient subject; the idea or representative object in perception to have no existence out of consciousness; and the idea and perception to be only different relations of a state of mind really the same.

Attention is not a simple mental state, but a combination of feelings. It is not a special faculty, nor the result of a special faculty, but is the result of the laws of perception, by which the increased vividness of one sensation produces a corresponding faintness in other coexisting sensations. The cause of this increased vividness is the *desire* of knowing connecting itself particularly with some one among our sensations, according to the general law by which our emotions give intensity to every perception with which they harmonize.

In treating of the Internal Affections of the Mind, Brown classes them all, as may be seen in the foregoing table, under two orders, Intellectual States and Emotions. These *Internal Affections* of the Mind are all resolved into Suggestion, or that constitutional principle of the mind by which the various mental states stand to each other in the relation of antecedence and consequence in a certain order. Brown repudiates the term Association of Ideas, because he conceives it to limit the facts included under it to *ideas*, whereas it should include emotions, sentiments, judgments, all the feelings of the mind. He considers, moreover, the natural constitution of the mind to be such, that not only one affection or state of it succeeds to another, and that the successions occur in a certain order, but also that the laws which regulate the recurrence are not laws of *association* in the strict sense of the term, as expressive of some former connecting process, but merely laws of *suggestion*, as expressive simply of the natural tendency of the mind, in the very moment when it is affected in a certain manner, to exist immediately afterward in a certain different state. This distinction Brown considers of great importance; and he adopts the term Suggestion not only as the simpler and more accurate expression for all the spontaneous successions of the mental states, but because otherwise we could explain but a part of the phenomena of the mind.

With this general view of suggestion, Brown proceeds to analyze all the Internal Affections of the Mind, which have commonly been ascribed to a variety of distinct powers or faculties, into Suggestion either Simple or Relative.

Simple Suggestion.—This comprehends all our conceptions or feelings connected with the past, and is that tendency by which the perception or conception of one object excites of itself, without any known cause external to the mind, the conception of some other object.

The laws of Simple Suggestion are Primary and Secondary. Of the Primary Laws Brown admits three: Resemblance, Contrast, and Nearness in Time or Place; though he is at the same time inclined to think they might all be resolved into one, which he terms a "fine species of proximity." The Secondary Laws are the most general circumstances which in various ways modify the primary laws

Importance is to be attached to the fact that the states of the mind which succeed each other, according to the laws of suggestion, do not merely *follow* each other, the suggesting state departing and giving way to the suggested state, but that it may remain, coexist, and blend with the other in a complex feeling.

Proceeding on these views, Brown attempts to resolve into forms of simple suggestion various phenomena of the mind which have been referred to distinct and special faculties.

1. *Conception.*—This has been defined the faculty by which we form a notion of an absent object of perception, or of some previous feeling of the mind. But there is no special faculty with this office. It is merely a particular determination of the general susceptibility of suggestion. When the sound of a friend's name is followed by the conception of his person, there are not two principles operating in the production of this mental state—a faculty of association and a faculty of conception—but only one, the principle of suggestion. We may call the state of mind a *conception*, in order to mark a more immediate reference to the object conceived ; and we may call it a *suggestion*, with more immediate reference to the conceiving mind ; but the latter is the principle of the phenomenon, and the only principle. The phenomenon is not to be referred to any special faculty of conception.

2. *Memory.*—Remembrances are only conceptions with which the notion of past time is connected, and may in like manner be analyzed, the first element of them into suggestion, as above, and the second element into a suggestion or feeling of relation. The notion of past time added to conceptions does not

require any new faculty or power of the mind distinct from the general principle of suggestion.—Recollection is only remembrance modified by *desire*.

3. *Imagination.*—This is no distinct faculty, but only the combination of conceptions or images according to the laws of suggestion. This combination may be spontaneous without the presence of desire, or it may be modified by desire in the way described in speaking of attention. When this latter is the case, it explains all that is implied in the voluntary shaping or creative imagination. Of the distinction between Fancy and Imagination Brown seems to have had no notion.

4. *Habit.*—This is not an original principle of the mind. The term expresses a tendency to the repetition of certain actions, and greater facility in performing them. This is resolvable into the general principle of suggestion, by which feelings tend to induce other feelings that have been before connected with them.

Relative Suggestion.—This comprehends all those feelings arising directly from previous feelings which suggest them, and to which they stand in some felt relation. These feelings of relation may all be classed under two heads: relations of coexistence, and relations of succession.

Relations of Coexistence.—To this class—which includes relations of real coexistence, as in matter, or of seeming coexistence, as in the complex phenomena of the mind—belong the relations of Position, Resemblance or Difference, Proportion, Degree, and Comprehension. These terms sufficiently explain the relations to which they apply. The perception or conception of objects, according as they stand in these relations, suggests the relations themselves.

The suggestions of resemblance and difference explain the formation of classes, the process of generalization, and explode all the controversy concerning universals between the Nominalists and Realists. The process of generalization and the formation of general terms is the following: 1. A perception of two or more objects; 2. A feeling of their resemblance; 3. The expression of this feeling of their relation by a word comprehending all the objects between which this relation exists. The general term expresses a state of mind entirely distinct from the primary perception of the individual objects.

This process of the mind may be misconceived and vitiated in two ways: by *adding* to it, or by *omitting*. To say that between the perception of two or more individual objects, comprehended by a general term and the feeling of their relation of resemblance, there intervenes some distinct substance, or some universal form distinct from the conceiving mind and from the individual objects, and that this produces the general notion to which the general term applies, is to err in the first way: it is the error of the Realists. To suppose that there is no intervening notion of general resemblance, no relative suggestion between the particulars and the formation of the general term, is to err in the second way: it is the error of the Nominalists.

The opinion of Brown as to the true process of generalization and the meaning of general terms, is regarded by him as essentially the same as that of Reid, and others called Conceptualists; whose incautious and incongruous language, and erroneous analysis of the general feeling, or feeling of resemblance, on which the whole process turns, have, however, served, in his opinion, to perplex the subject.

The process of *Reasoning* is likewise resolved into Relative Suggestion. Of the elements of reasoning, the general terms have been already explained. Propositions are only the verbal enunciation of the relation of two terms. All the relations may be expressed in propositions: there may be propositions of position, of resemblance, of proportion, of order, of degree, and of comprehension; to which last, indeed, all the others may be reduced. Every proposition expresses an analysis.

Reasoning, which consists of a number of propositions in a certain order, is only pursuing the analysis still farther, every step in the progress being only the analytic statement of what was contained in a prior comprehensive statement. However numerous the steps in the series, the last proposition is truly contained in the first. A new truth is not so much added as evolved.

Relations of Succession.—These include all our feelings which stand related to each other in the order of time. They may be casually prior and posterior when they occur as parts of different trains, or they may be invariably antecedent and consequent in a single train. The relations of cause and effect are resolved into suggestions of the latter sort.

There is no such special faculty as *Reason.* There is no ground for the distinction between Reason and Judgment. Reasoning is nothing more than a series of relative suggestions or feelings of relation, which, when expressed in words, form a series of propositions. To the susceptibility of feeling these relations, both the faculty called reason and the faculty called judgment may be alike reduced; the latter denoting the feeling of the relations of the terms of one proposition, the former of the series of propositions.

The process of *Abstraction* implies no special faculty. All the phenomena of the mind included in this term may be resolved either into the relative suggestion of resemblance or into simple suggestion, in which the partial representation of a concrete or complex whole may be suggested to the omission of the rest.

The Second Order of Internal Affections embraces the Emotions, which Brown has classified as immediate, retrospective, and prospective. He considers emotions to be distinguished from the intellectual states of the mind by a certain peculiar vividness of feeling, none the less readily recognised because it is undefinable. It is unnecessary to notice all the phenomena which Brown has comprehended in this order. Many of them belong properly and exclusively to this order of phenomena, and are accurately and beautifully analyzed. We shall confine our exposition to some special topics.

The term Beauty denotes an *emotion* in distinction from sensation. It is not the direct or immediate result of an affection of any organ of sense; it is a feeling distinct from, though connected with, the sensible perception of the object termed beautiful, just as hope, fear, etc., are distinct from the affections of the sensibility which precede and occasion them.

The term beauty denotes likewise exclusively an *emotion*, in opposition to the doctrine which makes beauty an object for any intellectual state of the mind, an object of judgment or reason.

Beauty is a mere general term, comprehensive of certain peculiar agreeable affections of the mind felt in reference to various objects. It is not anything existing independently of particular objects, nor is it any simple quality of those objects. It no more exists in objects, than species or genera exist in individuals. It is as absurd to inquire what constitutes the beautiful, as it is to inquire what constitutes the pleasing. Hence all theories which have attempted to decide what constitutes the beautiful, are as absurd as those which should attempt to resolve the pleasing exclusively into some particular sight, or taste, or smell. The term beautiful is wholly relative to our own minds. The objects which we call beautiful are such merely because the perception of them is followed by certain agreeable feelings. Yet the beautiful is not any quality inherent in the objects; least of all is it any common quality existing alike in all the different sorts and individuals of beautiful objects, and which is the ground of our being thus affected. Some philosophers have regarded beauty as something existing independently of particular objects, and manifested by them; others as a simple quality common to all objects called beautiful. These incorrect views have resulted from the peculiar vividness of the feeling, and from the natural tendency of the mind to attach its own feelings to the objects that occasion them.

The question why the feeling of beauty is connected with certain objects, Brown resolves by supposing an original tendency of the mind to be so affected by some objects, while as to another and larger class of objects it is the result of association.—The Sublime differs from the Beautiful only in degree.

In his *Ethical* system Brown resolves the essence of virtue into a certain vivid feeling or emotion of *approveableness.* Certain actions, or, rather, according to a distinction upon which he much insists, certain agents in certain circumstances excite in us immediately and irresistibly, from the constitution of our minds, the emotions of moral approbation. To the actions which awaken this emotion we give the generic name virtue, which denotes neither anything in itself, nor any simple quality of actions, but is a mere collective term to denote those actions which we find by experience do awaken this emotion. The fact that certain actions awaken the emotion constitutes their approveableness, and the virtue of the actions. This approveableness is but a relation of the action to the emotion. Virtue, obligation, merit, all mean essentially the same thing, differing only in respect to time. The irresistible feeling of approbation constitutes to us who consider the action, the virtue of the action itself, the obligation to perform it, and the merit of the performance. "Virtue," says Brown, "being a term expressive only of the relation of certain actions, as contemplated, to certain emotions in the minds of those who contemplate them, cannot, it is evident, have any universality beyond that of the minds in which these emotions arise. We speak always, therefore, relatively to the constitution of our minds, not to what we might have been constituted to admire . . . . . . and the supposed immutability, therefore [of moral distinctions], has regard only to the existing constitution of things under the Divine Being who has formed our social nature."

Observations.

The absorbing of all thought, all the faculties of the mind into consciousness, and consciousness itself into feeling, is the fundamental peculiarity of Brown's philosophy. This, with the principle of suggestion considered as a constitutional tendency or law of the mind regulating the combination and succession of feelings, involves his whole system: a system widely at variance, and in its most important points in absolute contradiction, with that of Reid and Stewart. With a strong natural bias of mind towards extreme simplification, his fundamental theory became with him an hypothesis to be applied to rather than a result obtained by an impartial, accurate, and complete observation of the phenomena of the mind. Hence, while we have many ingenious, beautiful, and often accurate analyses, we have also many, especially in regard to the fundamental questions of philosophy, in which the most important facts are overlooked, or distorted, or mutilated.

Hence he is led not only to deny the doctrine of Reid, that consciousness is a special distinct faculty, by which we become aware of the feelings of the mind, but also to deny that it is anything but the feelings themselves, thus confounding the condition of a fact with the fact itself. Because to be conscious at any particular moment implies some particular sensation, thought, or emotion of which we are conscious, he argues that the sensation, thought, or emotion is consciousness; because to be aware implies something to be aware of, therefore the being aware and the something whereof we are aware are the same thing: a conclusion as grossly illogical as it is contradictory to the best evidence which the subject admits, which is practically admitted every day, and which all goes to prove that for the mind to be affected, whether in sensibility, in thought, in volition, or emotion, is one thing, and to be conscious of it is another thing; and though the latter implies the former, the former by no means always implies the latter.

From the same systematic source, and sustained by a like gross paralogism, comes his confusion and identification of causation with succession. Because every cause is an invariable antecedent, therefore every invariable antecedent is a cause: a conclusion no less strangely violating the simplest rules of logic, than contradictory to the fundamental convictions of the mind, which decide that a cause is not only that which invariably *precedes*, but also that which *produces* the effect.

In the same systematic spirit, he denies the distinction between the primary and secondary qualities of matter, and confounds perception with sensation, and a suggested belief.

There is no external world as an object of perception: there are only sensations, and a belief invincibly suggested of their relation to some antecedent out of the mind.

The same excessive desire for systematic simplification is seen in his reduction of all the intellectual faculties to suggestion.

His mode of settling the controversy between Realism and Nominalism, which is peculiar, and in perfect harmony with his system, proceeds upon a misconception in respect to the error of both the doctrines. He saw very clearly that the Realists were wrong in asserting that there is a general essence independent of particular objects, answering to *every* general term; but, from the nature of his system, he did not see that to *some* general terms, as space, time, etc., there are general objects independent of particulars, to which they apply. He held the Nominalists to be wrong, because they attached the general term to particular objects without referring to the resemblance between the particulars: but the Nominalists did no such thing. They maintained that there are general terms, as quadruped, which refer to no general object apart from the individuals included under them; and herein Brown would agree they were right: but they also held the same of *every* general term; herein was their error: an error which Brown did not perceive, because it was also his own error. The question about Nominalism is not—as Brown takes for granted it is—a question whether there is or is not a felt relation of resemblance between individuals of the same kind, which leads to the formation of the general term, but whether the general term expresses any general object actually existing apart from individuals with common qualities.

Denying the Beautiful to be either anything in itself, which may be more or less represented by objects of perception, or any simple quality in the objects termed beautiful, Brown resolves it into a mere agreeable emotion of a peculiar kind. He thus confounds both the beautiful, and the perception and judgment of it, with a mere sentiment or affection of the sensibility which accompanies or follows the perception and judgment, and thereby destroys the possibility of any absolute standard of beauty or fixed rules of art.

The same general confusion corrupts the Moral system of Brown. Virtue is relative wholly to our constitution. Certain actions awaken emotions of approbation, just as certain flavours, etc., are naturally agreeable to the senses. It is supposable that our constitution might have been otherwise: and virtue and vice would have signified quite opposite actions from what they now signify. There is, then, no absolute, essential, and immutable difference between virtue and vice. The very immutability of moral distinctions affirmed by Brown is admitted by him to be relative to the human constitution.

According to Brown, we do not approve an action because it is virtuous, but it is virtuous because we approve it. This is contrary to the fact, and is a confusion of two distinct though inseparable things, the judgment of an act as right, and then an accompanying or consequent feeling of approbation. Brown admits that the actions which are now approved, and thereby made virtuous, might have been their very opposites, and that such is not our constitution is owing to the will of God. But why should God have so constituted us? We, it is true, on Brown's principles, *must* approve and disapprove as we do, because we are so formed: but can the same reason apply to God? In short, what other reason can be conceived why God should have formed us to approve a certain action as *right*, except that it *is* right in itself independently of our feeling?

MACKINTOSH.

SIR JAMES MACKINTOSH was born in Invernesshire, in Scotland, in 1765, and educated at Aberdeen. He afterward studied medicine at Edinburgh, and took his degree of doctor in 1787. The celebrity he acquired by his *Vindiciæ Gallicæ*, or Defence of the French Revolution against Burke, published in 1791, diverted his attention to politics, and led him to adopt the profession of law. He was appointed Recorder of Bombay in 1803, and resided in India till 1811. In 1813 he became a member of Parliament. He died in 1832. In his *General View of the Progress of Ethical Philosophy*, he has brought out a system of his own peculiar enough to merit a brief notice in this place.

Mackintosh opposes the selfish system, and believes in the reality of disinterested virtue: but he denies that our notions of right and wrong are original conceptions of our reason, or that reason can be the source of any principles which can influence the will. He agrees, therefore, with the advocates of the sentimental system and of the system of the moral sense, in making conscience a function of the sensibility. He differs from them, however, in denying that it is a primitive original principle: he thinks it is gradually formed and developed out of other and primitive affections, or, in his own language, is a principle of *secondary* formation, like self-love.

Self-love, the general desire for happiness, is not primitive; it presupposes certain original instinctive propensities, and the pleasure resulting from their gratification, and then this pleasure constructed by the mind as the object of desire, the end which it seeks. Self-love is thus a principle of secondary formation. So is it likewise with conscience. The painful or agreeable sentiment naturally attending certain emotions is transferred by association to the actions they produce, and thus the actions themselves become at length the immediate objects of approbation or repugnance. By the association of ideas, a number of secondary desires and aversions, which relate to actions or volitions, are combined in our minds, and form a sort of internal sense, which we call *conscience,* which approves or condemns certain actions or volitions in themselves, and without regard to their useful or injurious consequences. This conscience is the only affection of our nature whose immediate objects are volitions or voluntary actions. The power of this conscience over the will results from the instinctive influence of the primitive dispositions from which the moral sense is derived, from the pleasure naturally accompanying the development of those dispositions, and finally from the pleasure which likewise naturally accompanies a secondary desire.—By thus making conscience a *derived* sense, and making the essence of virtue to consist in the emotion or affection of that sense, the system of Mackintosh lies open to all the objections brought against those which resolve virtue into some primitive emotion or into the affection of an original sense: virtue becomes relative and contingent, and all real ground for the essential and absolute difference of right and wrong is destroyed.

COLERIDGE.

SAMUEL TAYLOR COLERIDGE was born in Devonshire in 1772, and died in 1834. He was educated first at Christ Church Hospital school, and afterward at Cambridge. In his early life he was a follower of Hartley; but at a later period, his philosophical, as well as his religious and political views, underwent a great change. He was a man of eminent genius as a poet and as a thinker, and was possessed of an immense amount of various and profound learning: but he was averse to regular and systematic production.

It is not as the founder of any complete and peculiar system that his name is here introduced. His philosophical writings are extremely fragmentary, consisting of scattered contributions to psychology, metaphysics, morals, politics, and æsthetics. These, though strongly marked by the author's profound learning, depth, and originality of mind, exhibit principles not fundamentally different from those of the great systems which have appeared in opposition to exclusive empiricism. To analyze or to reproduce his peculiar modes of establishing or illustrating these principles, would occupy too much space to be here given to writings which present no complete and peculiar system. Yet the great influence which Coleridge has exerted upon the character and direction of philosophical thinking, entitles his name to a place in the history of philosophy, and would make it improper to pass it by without, at least, some general remarks.

Coleridge represents himself to have devoted the largest part of his mature life to the preparation of a systematic work, which was to contain a full and complete exposition of his philosophy, and to have substantially executed a part of his plan. He did not live to publish any portion of this work. Of the philosophical writings published by him, the most general character is critical and polemical, as against the principles of sensualism in philosophy and of the selfish system in morals. Of these, in their principles and in their consequences, he was a most earnest opponent, and in various passages of his works he has placed the objections which may be urged against them in a very original and striking light.

Coleridge sketched a psychological classification of the phenomena of the mind under the following powers or faculties: the senses; the imitative power, voluntary and automatic; the imagination, or shaping and modifying power; the fancy, or aggregative and associative power; the understanding, or regulative, substantiating, and realizing power; the speculative reason, *vis theoretica et scientifica*, or the power by which we produce, or aim to produce, unity, necessity, and universality in all our knowledge, by means of principles *à priori;* the will, or practical reason; the faculty of choice; and (distinct both from the moral will and choice) the sensation of volition, which is included under the head of single and double touch.

Of the phenomena thus classified, he has, however, given no complete analysis; and, with the exception of some remarks upon the distinction between fancy and imagination, has explained his views distinctly upon none of them except the moral will and the understanding and reason. In regard to the will, he strenuously maintains it to be a self-determining power, not subject to the law of cause and effect, and holds this as the only possible ground of moral accountability.

The distinction between the understanding and the reason he insists upon as of the utmost consequence in its relations to all the higher questions of ontology, morals, and theology. These faculties, he contends, in the same way as Kant, are different in kind: the former being the faculty of judging according to sense, or the faculty of generalizing the notices received from the senses according to certain forms, and referring them to their proper names and classes; the latter being the faculty of originating, by occasion of notices of the senses, necessary and universal principles.

Some of the most interesting things in the writings of Coleridge relate to the differences and to the analogies between life and intelligence, and to the illustration which may be derived to psychology from the consideration of the dynamic forces. From these sources he has drawn many profound and original views, of great importance in their general bearing upon the mechanical philosophy and material psychology.

Coleridge borrowed largely from Kant and Schelling; and though, in reading his writings, the impression can hardly be resisted that he was equal to them in original speculative ability, and their superior in learning and critical power, yet, from his indolence, and his want of constructive talent, and particularly the talent for clear and systematic exposition, he has contributed little that will occupy a permanent and substantive place in the general history of philosophy. His writings contain numerous thoughts and fragments of thought, which may continue to be, as they have already been, rich germes, that may be unfolded by meditative minds endowed with more patience and skill in development than he possessed. In this way the influence of Coleridge has been very considerable in opposing the progress of a superficial and materializing spirit in philosophy, and in establishing the foundations of the great truths of morals and religion.

GERMAN PHILOSOPHY IN THE NINETEENTH CENTURY.

SCHELLING'S SYSTEM OF ABSOLUTE IDENTITY.

Historical Notices.

FREDERIC WILLIAM VON SCHELLING was born at Leonberg, in Wirtemberg, in 1775. He studied at Leipsic and at Jena. At the latter place he was a pupil of Fichte, whom he succeeded as professor there. In 1820 he removed to Erlangen, and lectured in the University. He was made secretary of the Academy of Fine Arts at Munich, and ennobled by the King of Bavaria. In 1827 he was appointed professor in the University of Munich. He published a great number of works, a few of which appeared in the last years of the eighteenth century.

Schelling was full of originality as a thinker; superior to Fichte in many respects, having a richer imagination, more poetic spirit, and a much greater extent of learning and information. He was at first a partisan of Fichte, whose system he defended against the Kantians; but he gradually separated himself from his master, and at length brought out a system of his own: a system so strange in substance and form, when compared with current philosophical ideas and language, that it is scarcely possible to give the general reader any intelligible account of it within the limits of a work like this. An attempt will, however, be made.

Exposition.

Fichte had deduced everything from the subjective as creating and containing all reality. Yet why may not the objective produce the subjective, as well as the subjective the objective? No reason can be given. We can no more deduce the infinite from the finite, than the finite from the infinite, by any of the processes of reflection. In order to have complete science, therefore, we must find a principle in which both the finite and infinite, the subjective and objective, are originally united. This principle is the Absolute Identity of subject and object in cognition. In Absolute Identity, knowing and being are one. The absolute in itself contains the essence and the form of all things. The absolute and its development constitute all reality. The absolute in itself is neither being nor knowing, neither infinite nor finite, but the ground of both.

All the phenomena of the universe are the development of the absolute identity either in the direction of the ideal or of the real, that is, either as the thinking principle or as objects of thought; just as all the phenomena of magnetism are the results of one identical force manifesting itself in opposite poles. The absolute identity of being and knowing manifests itself sometimes with a predominance of the ideal, sometimes of the real. This development of the absolute is apprehended by a process which Schelling sometimes calls Intellectual Intuition, sometimes a spontaneous revelation of the absolute, and sometimes a descent or fall of ideas from the absolute.

Conformably with these views, the following are the leading propositions of this system:

1. There exists but one sole, substantial, identical Being. Finite existences, or objects produced by reflection, which is altogether relative in its nature, have only an apparent reality.

2. The absolute Being reveals himself in the eternal generation of things, which constitute the forms and modes of this sole and only Being. Everything is therefore a manifestation of God under a determinate form, and nothing can exist which does not partake of the Divine Being. Nature accordingly is not dead, but living and divine equally with the spiritual world.

3. The manifestation of the absolute being in opposite directions, like that of the polar forces in nature, which are but different expressions of one identical force, there are various degrees of development, the ideal sometimes predominating, and sometimes the real. Science is the investigation of this development; it is an image of the universe.

This ideal construction of the universe, according to which all plurality and diversity are regarded only as a relative form of absolute identity, may be thus exhibited:

I. The ABSOLUTE, the WHOLE, in its first form (GOD) manifests itself in

II. NATURE (the Absolute in its second form).

It therein projects itself in two orders of the Relative, to wit:

The Real.	The Ideal.
Under the following powers:	
Gravity—Matter.	Truth—Science.
Light—Motion.	Goodness—Religion.
Organization—Life.	Beauty—Art.

As reflected forms of the universe, we have,

Man (the Microcosm) . . . . The State.
The System of the World (the external Universe) . History.

In this way, by Intellectual Intuition, Schelling believed he had discovered in ideas both the essence and the necessary form of things. Thus he imagined he had corrected the error of Kant, who admitted only a subjective notion of the phenomenal world, and a simple belief in the reality of things in themselves; and thus, also, he pretended to refute Fichte, who made the thinking principle the sole reality, and nature a non-reality, a mere limit or negative of the absolute activity of the thinking principle.

Schelling applied his fundamental principles chiefly to the philosophy of nature, treating of the ideal branch only in respect to some special questions in his later writings.

In morals, he taught that the belief in God is the primary basis of morality. The existence of a moral world immediately follows from the existence of God.

Morality is the necessary tendency of the soul to unite itself to its centre, to God. Virtue is conformity to this tendency. Virtue and happiness are identical.

The social life, regulated conformably to the Divine type in respect to morals, religion, science, and art, is social order, or the State.

History, in its totality, is a progressive and unceasing revelation of God.

In his treatise on the freedom of man, Schelling distinguishes God, conceived in the perfect purity of the idea, or as the absolute, from God as existent or revealing himself, in which latter relation he evolves himself out of the absolute God, in virtue of a principle contained in himself, a nature in God, and thus comes to the state of complete existence; so that it is in the world that God comes to a state of personality. *Deus implicitus explicitus.* God is the absolute identity of the ideal and real evolving itself from the original absolute union, or, rather, confusion, or, adopting an image from dynamics, indifference of both.

There is a like double principle in every being produced by nature.

In man this principle is personality, which is composed of reason and will. When personality acts arbitrarily, in opposition to reason, which is the proper law of freedom, evil arises, which, however, is only relative.

The Beautiful, which Schelling treats only in relation to works of art, is the representation of the infinite by the finite. Creative art is an expression of ideas; it is a revelation of God in the human mind.

Observations.

1. Schelling aimed to give a complete philosophy of the universe, to deduce and explain all things from speculative principles. His system reduces everything to a single idea, and thereby maintains the possibility for man of a certain knowledge, not only of the subjective, but also of the objective, on the ground that the human mind and God are primitively identical. It thus destroys the chasm between the finite and infinite, which philosophy, unwilling to leap it by faith, has ever been attempting to bridge.

It removes likewise all distinction between empirical and rational cognition, between knowledge given in experience and knowledge given in the necessary laws of reason; it thus makes speculative principles equally the basis of all the sciences.

2. Yet the whole system is destitute of a solid ba

sis. It sets out, not from a fact of consciousness, but from Intellectual Intuition, a mere assumption neither self-evident nor demonstrable.

Again, thought without a thinking subject is a pure abstraction ; absolute identity cannot be conceived without a relative identity ; for without this condition the Absolute reduces itself to Nothing. The alleged original confusion of thought and the nature of things is a mere abstraction ; and in pretending that it represents reality and the nature of things, a hypothesis without proof is set up.

3. This system is more scientific in appearance than in reality. Schelling's problem was to deduce by a real demonstration the finite from the infinite, the relative from the absolute, the particular from the universal. This is a problem which cannot be solved, and Schelling has not solved it. His demonstrations consist of assertions and assurances, supported by analogies, images, and notions borrowed from experience.

4. The idea of God presented in this system is both in itself and in its most important relations, objectionable. God is subjected to a blind destiny, under which he must evolve himself from non-intelligence to intelligence, from a nature in God to God. This is a mere hypothesis, and, besides, neither accounts for the existence of God, nor renders it any more comprehensible than the common theory, which supposes him to have existed from eternity as the All-perfect Being : a theory which can never be disproved.

It is, also, a system of pantheism in one sense of the word : it identifies nature with God, and asserts the immanence of all things in him ; thus destroying all proper notion of the creation and government of the world by infinite wisdom and holiness. It destroys the substantial individuality and personality of creatures, and all freedom of will in man, and thereby contradicts the law of duty in conscience, and destroys the distinction between right and wrong.

Progress of the School of Schelling.

The system of Schelling was attractive by the apparent facility with which it offered to explain the universe; by its many novel and striking ideas; by the prospect which it held out of the indefinite extension of human knowledge; and particularly by its contrast with the dry forms of Kant, and the lifeless system of Fichte. With many the attraction was, perhaps, increased by the very faults of the author's method and style: his obscure and fluctuating terminologies, and his mystical expressions and images imitated from Plato. These circumstances, combined with the spirit of his time and of the German mind, may perhaps explain the enthusiasm excited by the philosophy of Schelling. A numerous school was formed among philosophers, theologians, philologists, physicians, and naturalists. All branches of science were treated in the spirit of his system. The ideas of Schelling exerted especially a great influence upon physical inquiries, upon mythology, history, and the theory of the arts and criticism, in the latter of which the celebrated brothers Schlegel, at that time associates and friends of Schelling, contributed powerfully to extend the influence of his system.

On the other hand, this school was prolific in fantastic ideas and mystical extravagances, which almost revived the age of New-Platonism.

Of the numerous writers who belong to the school of Schelling, our limits forbid our speaking in detail. Many of them endeavoured to reconcile his system with Revelation and Christianity; others did not deny their incompatibility. Of his early followers, some, as Eschenmayer and Wagner, became afterward his opponents; others modified his system in some respects; and Hegel put forth a different system. Of those who confined themselves to expounding and teaching the system of Schelling, the most faithful interpreter was *Klein*, professor at Wurtzburg, who died in 1820. It was reduced to didactic forms by *Thanner* and *Rixner*, and its principles were applied to theology by *Daub*. To these might be added a long list of writers who have developed or modified this system, or parts of it, in various degrees and applications; but it would be of little use to cite their names, and we should have room for nothing more.

Among the opponents of the philosophy of Schelling may be mentioned all the principal partisans of the system of Kant (the most distinguished of whom are *Fries* and *Krug*); the authors of some new systems, as *Herbart, Bardili, Bouterwek*, and *Jacobi* and his school. Various other attempts to construct the system of philosophy were put forth in the first years of the present century; but they are either too eccentric and obscure, or too superficial to deserve attention; and as to the rest, they are mostly the ideas of others, having a character of novelty only from their peculiar nomenclature. Of the writers that have been named, we shall briefly notice Bouterwek and the school of Jacobi.

BOUTERWEK.

Frederic Bouterwek, professor at Göttingen, born in 1766, died in 1828, was a distinguished thinker, though his acuteness too often degenerated into an obscure subtlety, notwithstanding the habitual clearness of his style. At first a follower of Kant, he became convinced that his philosophy could not be maintained against skepticism. The system of Fichte appeared too exclusive to satisfy the desire for reality in the mind; and, on the other hand, it seemed to him that science cannot dispense with the absolute, without which he could not conceive the possibility of knowledge or thought, since in all our proofs we always suppose something real, an entity, the absolute, that unknown *X*, which, according to Kant, subsists under all phenomena. Bouterwek therefore proposed, in his *Idea of a Universal Apodictic*, to supply the defects and correct the vices of anterior systems, which he found fault with as investigating our cognitions and beliefs only in notions of the understanding and empty formulas, and consequently never attaining to any living fundamental science.

The doctrine of this work may be reduced to the following points:

All our sensations and thoughts have for their basis a true existence, consequently an absolute existence, having its basis only in itself. This existence cannot be found and demonstrated by thought, since all thought presupposes it, and being is superior to thought. Consequently, either existence must be reduced to a caprice of the imagination, and all thought to a chimera, or there must be a faculty of absolute cognitions, which is neither sensation nor thought: a faculty upon which rests the authenticity of reason itself, and by which we arrive directly (apodictically) at all existence.

Subsequently Bouterwek abandoned this *apodictic*, and substituted for it a new scheme: one which he called a Universal Theory of Truth and Science, according to which, on the principle of the *faith of rea-*

son in itself, he constructed a less bold system of transcendental rationalism. In this view, the principal object of philosophy is to solve, by the apodictical distinction of the real and the apparent, the problem of things and the destination of man, as far as it is possible for human reason to penetrate by itself this question. It is therefore upon an *apodeictic* (according to the last view adopted by Bouterwek) that philosophy must be grounded: empirical psychology and logic, ordinarily understood as the science of the forms of thought, can furnish only the preliminary notions. Here the author agrees with Jacobi, that all purely logical thinking is mediate. All our immediate cognitions, without which we could conceive of a discursive notion only as mediate, and consequently uncertain, rest upon the primitive bond of connexion of the thinking faculty with an internal sentiment in the energy of the spiritual life, that is, in the unity of the active faculties of our being, as well subjective as objective. Reason has faith in itself as far as it is pure reason; it believes in the truth, inasmuch as it recognises in it, in virtue of the bond of connexion just indicated, its own peculiar and original energy, and in that same energy finds the germe of ideas, by the aid of which it can rise above the sphere of the sensibility, and investigate the principle of all existence and all thought, or the idea of the absolute. Truth, in the metaphysical sense of the word, is the agreement of our thoughts with the supersensible essence of things, and their necessary relation to the principle of all being and all thought: truth is therefore immediately known by reason. To give this idea a scientific form, by showing how, upon what grounds, and to what extent, a positive knowledge of things is possible for the human mind, is the province of metaphysics (including religious philosophy grounded in the religious sentiment). Bouterwek applied his principles to a system of morals and natural law, and attempted also to form a system of æsthetics upon purely psychological principles.

New Developments of the Philosophy of Sentiment.

JACOBI has already been mentioned, in connexion, with Kant, as one who exerted a powerful influence in the reaction against the Critical philosophy. But it should be added that he lived till 1819, and no less vigorously opposed the subsequent developments of speculation as they appeared in the systems of Fichte and Schelling. Dissatisfied with the Critical philosophy, as taking away all rational ground for belief in supersensible things, and equally dissatisfied with all dogmatical systems of speculation, which, if consistent, can only lead to fatalism or pantheism, and yet unable to find solid ground in the idea of a supernatural revelation, he continued to ground all philosophical knowledge upon a sort of rational instinct, an immediate sentiment or direct apperception of supersensible truth. This sentiment, this instinctive faith (quite distinct from positive historical faith in revelation), gives us the knowledge of the external world, of God, of Providence, of Freedom, Immortality, Morality: in short, the whole supersensible order of things, in virtue of an internal sense, an organ of truth, to which he afterward gives the name of reason, or the faculty of cognition.

Some obscurity in which he left his fundamental principle, and some want of precision in the distinction he made between reason as the faculty of supersensible ideas and understanding as the faculty of logical forms, exposed him to numerous misconceptions and attacks on the part of those whom he opposed. He found, however, numerous partisans, and may be said to have founded a school. But the vagueness to which we have alluded gave rise to a sort of schism among his followers.

Some of them considered ideas as divine revelations, by means of perception, and they attributed these ideas to reason as their special faculty: they held, moreover, that the notions of the understanding perform, with relation to these ideas, a part altogether negative; that is to say, that ideas could neither be attained, conceived, nor expressed by the aid of notions of the understanding; that they are manifested in sentiment alone; in fine, that faith precedes and surpasses all science.

Others conceded more to logical notions, and made philosophy consist in the unity of reason and understanding: a unity which takes its substance from reason, and its form from understanding. This second opinion was adopted by Jacobi himself, but only in his latter years.

The first of these views was maintained by *Frederic Kœppen*, a genial writer, and the author of an excellent exposition of the system of this school. To the second class of opinions belong the works of *James Salat.*

Kœppen, the friend and disciple of Jacobi, sets out with the idea of freedom: according to him, freedom is a causative power, which takes its determination in itself, without any determining principle, and independently of any relation; it is consequently the first cause, the ground of all existence; in short, Being properly called. But, at the same time, freedom is altogether inconceivable by the understanding; even its possibility cannot be distinctly apprehended, nor its reality demonstrated; it is a fact of cognition and of activity perceived immediately. Necessity is an order established by freedom. To speak of unlimited and absolute freedom is to speak of the divine power. But the nature of human individuality consists in the relation of the internal and external. By this relation freedom is found to be limited in man. All philosophy is consequently a *dualism*. On this dualism turns the everlasting and inevitable contradiction of science. From this, again, it follows that philosophy, strictly speaking, is impossible, and that all scientific pretension in the proper sense of the word, all pretension to a speculative system that shall embrace both the finite and the infinite, is destined only to fall back foiled upon itself.

The writings of Kœppen, as well as those of Jacobi, whatever be thought of their system in its fundamental principles, exerted a very salutary influence upon the philosophy of the day. They opposed the rashness of dogmatic speculation; they developed with great freshness and spirit many valuable ideas, some original, some borrowed from Platonism; and their very inability to substitute anything adequately satisfying to the moral wants of the mind, in place of the speculative systems they opposed, tended to recall men to a positive faith, grounded in a higher source than their principle of sentiment. It may be added that Jacobi himself is said before his death to have admitted the authority of revelation as the source of the knowledge of divine things.

NOTE.

The most recent German Speculations. Hegel.

It would be scarcely possible to give within the limits of this sketch anything like a clear and complete view of the progress of philosophy in Germany for the last twenty years, or of its present condition.

While Fries, Krug, and some others continued to maintain the principles of Kant, and the school of Jacobi to oppose all dogmatic speculations, new developments and modifications, in various directions, of the principles of Schelling from time to time appeared, until at length philosophical discussion received a new direction from the attempt of Hegel to establish a system distinct from any of the preceding.

George Will. Fred. HEGEL was born in 1770. He was professor successively at Jena, Heidelberg, and Berlin, at which latter place he died of the cholera in 1831.

Hegel was at first the disciple of Schelling, and, as such, published in 1801 a tract on the difference between the systems of Fichte and Schelling. He was also associated with him in the conduct of a philosophical journal in 1802–3. But his opinions gradually took a different turn. He rejected Schelling's Intellectual Intuition as an unwarrantable assumption, although he continued to maintain its grounding idea, namely, the unity of the subjective or ideal, and the objective or real; and in this idea endeavoured to establish that absolute cognition and absolute truth, which alone, according to this school, can satisfy the demands of the philosophical spirit. Hence he maintained that pure conception in itself, and pure conception alone, is true being, without having, however, demonstrated this identity of being and thinking. Equally arbitrary, also, is the position that everything rational is real, and everything real rational: a position which, in a practical view, would make the moral law, considered as demands of the reason upon the will, without object, and therefore superfluous, since the will, by the terms of the position, can make nothing real that is not rational.

The weakest part of the system of Hegel is the

æsthetical, or philosophy of art, and the theological, or philosophy of religion. It is said by Weisse, once a very warm partisan of Hegel, but since somewhat cooled, that æsthetics and theology begin where Hegel leaves off. For what we call the ideas of the Beautiful and of God, Hegel admits only in the way of psychological and historical appearance; they are to him merely phenomenal, and the science of them is merely a part of the phenomenology of the mind.

Hegel seems not, indeed, to have perfectly developed his system; and as he was very deficient in the talent for exposition, and his writings are not only extremely obscure, but dry and harsh, it is scarcely possible to be satisfied that one has a clear and complete view of his philosophy. Of those who would be thought to comprehend it, very many regard it as a perfect system of rational science. Certain it is that he exerted a powerful influence on the German mind; he founded a school, and drew around him a numerous body of zealous and distinguished followers. He derived, indeed, external support from a prevalent impression that his system tended better than any other to secure the permanence of the existing order of things in Church and State, and this political popularity increased the number of his disciples. Some eight or ten years since, it was said by one of Hegel's critics to be a remarkable thing, that among his numerous disciples, none had yet been able to relieve the obscurity, heaviness, and dryness of his mode of philosophizing by a clearer, more agreeable, and lively exposition; that they all continued to use their master's words, phrases, and turns of expression, as if they were magic formulas, which would lose their power by the slightest change. The case would seem since then to have become somewhat otherwise, in some respects at least; for while a portion of his followers continue to adhere to the more abstruse and speculative forms and style of Hegel, others are endeavouring to popularize and extend it in every direction. A schism appears, indeed, to have sprung up in the bosom of the school, which, joined with the powerful attacks made upon it from without, chiefly in the interest of religion and morals, would seem to betoken the dissolution and downfall of which Hegel is said, shortly before his death, to have expressed a presentiment. At present it is the centre of nearly all philosophical interest. Its principles, particularly in their applications to theology and morals, as developed and defended by its friends, and opposed by its enemies, are subjects of the most animated controversy. Some of Hegel's school endeavour to reconcile his principles with orthodox Christianity; others impose them upon Christianity, giving its historical documents only a mythical or allegorical significance; while others reject it altogether, and openly proclaim opinions at variance with all ordinary notions of religion or morality.

The system of Hegel, equally with that of Schelling, is charged with being a species of pantheism. That it may be so is to be inferred, not merely from its pretension of giving the knowledge of the absolute, but from its identification of the subjective and objective. Some of the followers of Hegel assert the personality of God; but others expressly deny it, and maintain that they only are in harmony with Hegel. God is represented by them as the immanence of spirit in the world; as an eternal, universal principle, manifesting itself in individual existences, having no objective existence but in those individuals; coming to self-consciousness only in human reason, and having no personality distinct from the personality of man. They are also represented as holding that the Absolute attains to consciousness in a series of individuals, no one of which perfectly represents him, each having significance only as a member of the whole.

It is needless to dwell upon the consequences of pantheism as a part of the system thus represented, the subversion of all proper ideas of morality, human freedom, immortality, and another world. Whether or not Hegel admitted these consequences, one of his most respectable followers shows that some of the most important of them are logically involved in his principles, and all of them are expressly maintained by others.—Such is a very imperfect sketch of the present state of philosophical discussion in Germany.

FRENCH PHILOSOPHY IN THE NINETEENTH CENTURY.

Preliminary Observations.

It has already been seen how, in the latter half of the eighteenth century, the principles of Locke were unfolded in France by Condillac into a complete system of sensualism, and carried out by Helvetius, D'Holbach, and others to their legitimate consequences, materialism, fatalism, atheism, and the destruction of moral distinctions. From this time to the French revolution sensualism was the reigning doctrine; it pervaded every department of intellectual production, art, morals, religion, the physical and economical sciences. It extended itself from Paris throughout the provinces, and obtained complete control of the education of the country.

During the Revolution all minds were absorbed by the exciting events of that period, and the little phil osophical activity that existed was directed to political theories. With the restoration of public order the philosophical spirit began to awaken, and naturally enough continued in the direction in which it was proceeding when arrested. The philosophy of Condillac was revived, and, favoured by the organization of the Institute, and the establishment of the Normal Schools under the Directorial government, acquired a predominating influence. From this time to the Consulate philosophy was zealously cultivated, though always in the direction of sensualism. No opposition as yet had appeared, except incidentally in literary works. Among the most important works produced during this period are those of Cabanis and Destutt de Tracy.

From the time of the Empire tokens of a reaction began to appear more distinctly, though at first in productions of imagination and sentiment rather than scientific works. A more direct token and cause of the decline of sensualism consisted in the character of a work produced about this time by Laromiguiere, a writer avowedly of the school of Condillac, but who, by the distinctions he introduced, favoured a contrary system. But it was not until 1811 that the opposition to sensualism became organized and systematic. From 1811 to 1814 the celebrated Royer-Collard expounded the philosophy of Reid, and exerted a powerful influence in overthrowing the system of Condillac, and establishing a contrary system. The reaction against sensualism was still farther strengthened by a class of writers in the interest of religion and the Church, such as Le Maistre, Chateaubriand, Bonald, etc.

Thus, from the Empire to the Restoration, sensualism continued to decline, and from the latter period to the present day it may be said to have lost all authority and influence. The disciples and successors of Royer-Collard have completed the victory begun by him, and gone forward into a still wider sphere of speculation. For more than twenty years nearly all the leading minds have been on the side of the new movement, and the influence of a spiritual philosophy has pervaded French literature in almost every department.

A little more particular account of the principal writers connected with this revival and decline of sensualism, and with the progress of the new movement, will now be given.

SENSUAL SCHOOL

CABANIS.

Peter John George Cabanis was born at Cognac in 1757. He studied at Paris, where he addicted himself at first to general literature, but afterward to medical science. He was a member of the Institute, clinical professor in the medical school of Paris, and snbsequently a senator under the Empire. He died in 1808. His most important work, *Rapports du Physique and du Moral de l'Homme,* On the Relation of the Physical Organization of Man to his Moral Faculties (Paris, 1802), attracted great attention.

Exposition.

Cabanis grounded his views upon the system of Condillac, which explained all the phenomena of the mind by sensations. He adopted this system, and thought he could perfect and complete it by establishing the nature and origin of sensation itself.

It is not certain that among all animals sensation, or rather sensibility, is a property of the nerves: for there are some animals, as the polypi and infusorial insects, who have feeling, and yet are apparently destitute of any nervous apparatus. But in animals that resemble man, and in man especially, sensibility resides exclusively in the nerves, as the simple experiment of cutting or tying the trunk of any set of nerves demonstrates.

Sensation, moreover, depends upon every impression made upon the extremities of any set of nerves being followed by a reaction from the centre of the organ towards the extremities, so that sensibility unfolds itself in two distinct stages. In the first it acts, in the second it reacts; in the first it flows back from the circumference to the centre, and in the second returns from the centre to the circumference.

In whatever way this may be conceived, it is certain that sensibility resides in the nerves, and thereby all the moral faculties, intelligence, will, etc. Man is a moral being only because he is a sensitive being; he is sensitive only because he has nerves: man is entirely constituted by nerves. These are the principles unfolded in the work of Cabanis.

The extreme simplicity of the system is the first point with which one is struck. An impression received, an action and reaction of the nerves, a sentiment resulting: this is the whole theory. The relations between the physical and moral in man no longer offer any difficulties; the intellectual and moral faculties are the effect, the physical nervous organization the cause; sentiment or feeling is at once the last term of the phenomena which constitute life, and the first of those which we attribute to mind.

It is remarkable, again, with what ease this theory submits to a multitude of particular applications. It is well known, for instance, that age, sex, temperament, regimen, climate, exert a great influence on the intellectual and moral character of men: nothing is more easily explained; these are only so many circumstances affecting the nervous system, and through that the sensibility, intelligence, will, etc. Only get at the causes which act upon the state of the nerves, and the feelings that result from them, and you may easily explain all the moral phenomena of the human soul.

Observations.

1. But all this does not establish the truth of the theory of Cabanis. That in the present state of human existence a nervous organization and nervous impressions are the necessary condition of all intellectual and moral phenomena, may be readily admitted, and is certainly true; but it does not follow that they are their constituent principle and cause. So also it may be admitted that the nervous organization exercises a great influence in modifying intellectual and moral development, and yet it does not follow that the intellectual and moral in man result from this organization. In short, the facts established by Cabanis prove nothing against the distinct existence, the substantial nature, the unity and simplicity of the soul, as a principle different in itself from the organization, though at present intimately connected with it, and conditioned by it in regard to its activity.

2. The theory of Cabanis is burdened by insuperable difficulties. In the first place, it is impossible to explain how feeling should result from the action and reaction of the nerves. We can conceive that the first can take place, that the external object can excite an action (affection) of the nerve; but no principle is shown that is to produce the reaction. In the second place, if the nerves themselves feel

and are conscious, there is no way of explaining the *unity* of consciousness, which is nevertheless a fact of experience. For, according to the theory, there must be as many *selves* as there are different kinds of nervous impressions. It is to no purpose to say that the different nerves and their various affections all unite in a central organ, and thus produce our consciousness of unity, of our being one and the same self. This is merely taking a verbal for a real unity. For this nervous centre is only a collection of nerves designated by a common name.

3. It is needless to remark at length upon the moral consequences of this theory. It is a system of materialism, and, as such, involves fatalism, and the destruction of moral distinctions, of the belief in a future life and in God. Cabanis himself did not derive these consequences, and did not wish to hold them.

It may be added that the views of Cabanis were considerably modified at a later period, as appears from a letter of his published after his death. In his first work he did not consider the soul as a principle by itself; in this letter he no longer regards it as a result of the organization, but as a distinct living force present in the organization.

DESTUTT DE TRACY.

Count Destutt de Tracy, peer of France, was born in 1754. His *Elements of Ideology* were published in 1801.

He was the metaphysician of the sensual school of that period, as Cabanis was its physiologist. Cabanis, though a sensualist, and holding the principle of Condillac, occupied himself with it less as a philosopher than as a naturalist, desirous to explain the principle by a physiological hypothesis. De Tracy implicitly adopts the principle of Cabanis without analyzing or unfolding it. His object is to analyze all mental phenomena into sensation. Assuming his grounding principles from Condillac, he reasons from them with great strictness and with remarkable clearness of style.

His theory is very simple. The mind is nothing but sensibility. The sensibility is susceptible of four sorts of impressions: 1. Those which arise from the *present* action of objects upon the organs; 2. Those which result from their *past* action, by means of a certain disposition which that action left upon the organs; 3. Those of things which have *relations*, and may be compared; 4. Those which spring from our wants, and lead us to seek satisfaction for them. Everything comes from the affection of the sensibility through *impressions* made upon the organs of sense. When the sensibility is affected by the *first* sort of impressions, it *feels* simply; when by the *second*, it repeats or *recollects;* when by the *third*, it feels relations or *judges;* when by the *fourth*, it desires or *wills*. Thus sensation, according to the nature of its objects, manifests itself respectively as pure perception, or memory, or judgment, or will. It is, therefore, the sole principle of all our faculties, and of all operations of the mind, since there is none of them which may not be reduced to one or the other of these forms of sensibility.

With respect to the fundamental principle of De Tracy, the general objections that have been indicated in regard to Cabanis, Condillac, etc., apply of course. With respect to the particular analysis by which he has endeavoured to explain all mental phenomena according to that principle, it may be enough briefly to remark, that there are operations of the mind which cannot be explained by his method. *Generalization*, for example, is neither perception, nor recollection, nor judgment, nor volition, though it may presuppose them all. *Imagination* likewise, though conditioned by perception and aided by memory, is different from either; its function is to represent something that has never precisely existed for sensation. So, also, in regard to all the absolute, necessary, and universal convictions of the mind, they are presupposed in experience (sensation); they are suggested by it and applied to it; but they are never facts of sensation. By no analysis can the absolute conviction of the relations of the angles of all possible triangles to two right angles, of the relation of all possible phenomena to a cause, etc., be made facts of sensation. The same remark applies in regard to moral and religious ideas; and, finally, to select another example, without intending a complete enumeration, his confusion of will with desire, and reduction of all volitions to sensitive desires, contradicts our consciousness. If there are volitions (in his sense of the word) which he can explain as particular movements of the mind in sensation, there are others which he cannot so explain.

VOLNEY.

CONSTANTINE FRANCIS CHASSE-BŒUF, COUNT DE VOLNEY, was born at Craon, in Brittany, in 1755. Inspired from his youth with an ardent desire of seeing foreign countries, he travelled in Egypt and Syria, and studied the Oriental languages for some time at the convent on Mount Lebanon. He was a deputy of the *tiers etat* in the States-General in 1789, where he embraced the popular side. In 1794 he was professor of history at the normal school. He afterward travelled in the United States. Under the

Consulate he was a member of the senate. After the restoration in 1814 he was made a peer of France. He died in 1820. His most celebrated work is his *Ruins*, an infidel production. He is connected with the history of philosophy in France by his *Citizen's Catechism*, or *Physical Principles of Morals*. He is the moral philosopher of the sensual school of his time.

There is very little originality in his moral philosophy. It is essentially that of all the partisans of the sensual system; in particular, it is that of Helvetius, D'Holbach, and Saint-Lambert. Volney has only reduced it to its simplest expression.

His principle is clear and simple. *Self-preservation, to take care of his life*, is man's only duty. By this he means nothing profound, refined, or out of the ordinary sense. He understands the words as all the world understand them. He means that man should take care to preserve his life, to maintain himself in a sound physical state. Even if he were not explicit, the general system of philosophy which he adopted would remove all doubt. A partisan of the physiological theory of the sensual school, man was for him a collection of nervous organs; he had no soul, or, what comes to the same thing, his soul was nothing but a result of organized matter; there could, of course, be no other self-preservation, no other end of human actions, than to maintain the functions of life in a sound condition; no other duty than to follow the rules which tend to this end. Volney was not a man to be frightened at this consequence of his principle; he goes to it without flinching, and proclaims it without circumlocution. The applications are equally simple and clear. Good and evil, right and wrong, are easily determined. Moral good, right, is nothing but what tends to preserve and to improve the physical organization; moral evil, wrong, is nothing but what tends to destroy or impair it. The greatest good is life, the greatest evil is death; nothing is superior to physical enjoyment, nothing worse than bodily pain: the supreme good is health.

Vice and virtue are and can be only the voluntary habit of actions conformed or contrary to the law of taking care of one's organization. Particular virtues and vices in the individual, domestic, and social relations are determined by the same criterion.

In the particular application of his principles, Volney cannot be charged with doing violence to received moral opinions. Those things that he lays down as virtues are truly virtues: temperance, cleanliness; chastity, industry, economy, contentment; honesty, veracity, kindness: and the contrary of these he rightly denominates vices. His error is in the principle and motive on which he grounds their nature and obligation, namely, their adaptation to promote physical health and long life. Considered as prudential maxims subordinated to a higher principle, his practical ethics would be faultless as far as it goes; but as actually exhibited by him, it is not only incomplete, for there are obligatory practical maxims which cannot be analyzed into maxims of wellbeing, but also, as before said, corrupt in principle; for the ground of our obligation to honesty or veracity, for instance, is not their tendency to promote tranquillity, and thereby good health; they are obligatory apart from these consequences, and in special cases may entail opposite consequences, and yet be equally obligatory. In short, in common with all the selfish systems, by erecting a partial and contingent criterion into a universal maxim, and confounding that maxim with the principle of virtue, he destroys the essence itself of all virtue.

GALL, AZAIS, AND OTHER WRITERS.

The only other names of any note in the sensual school of the present century in France, are those of Garat, Lancelin, Broussais, Gall, and Azaïs. The writings of the first two offer nothing special. BROUSSAIS was a celebrated physiologist, and contended strongly for the sensual and materialist system against the new spiritual views that had then become predominant. His work on Irritability and Madness was published in 1828.

The celebrated Dr. GALL (born in 1758, died in 1828), though more properly ranked with the sensual school than with any other, was yet the founder of a system entirely his own. He holds, indeed, the fundamental principle of sensualism, that all our faculties are derived from the organization; and he agreed with the physiologists of that school in regarding the brain as the productive source of all our faculties. But he did not consider the brain as a single organ, but an assemblage of many distinct and special organs, whose locality and functions he minutely described; and from the relative size, activity, and mutual influence of which he explained all the intellectual and moral phenomena of man. This system was subsequently greatly developed, modified, and extended by Spurzheim, and has been, and continues still to be, zealously propagated under the name of phrenology. It is not necessarily a scheme of materialism; for, though it may be held in the materialist sense that all the phenomena of the mind are produced by these cerebral organs, it may also be held in the spiritualist sense that these organs are only the conditions and instruments of the manifestation of a spiritual principle distinct from them, though connected with them. As to the rest, it is not worth while here to go into an examination of the exclusive pretensions made in behalf of the system of phrenology. Its true things are no new things, and its new things (so far as they are of any importance to the proof of the system) have not yet been sufficiently proved to be true things.

Azais was born in 1766. He belongs in strictness to no school. His doctrine is peculiar to himself. He is here put in connexion with the sensual school, from the materialist character of his system in a moral point of view. He unfolded his system in lectures, delivered during the period of the Empire to crowded and brilliant audiences with great distinction and success; he also gave his views to the public through the press. His system is a peculiar physical explanation of the universe. Matter, the substance of being, is the passive subject of a universal action or movement impressed by God. This universal action has but one sole mode, *expansion;* every material substance is pervaded throughout by a force which tends to indefinite enlargement of the space it fills, and thereby to dissolution.

But this dissolution of each body is prevented by the same indefinite force of expansion acting in all other bodies in the universe. Hence a force of *repression* or conservation, which results from the very aw of universal *expansion.* By this force the heavenly bodies, their relations and motions, the earth, its various bodies and their properties, are explained; so, also, all organized beings, with their various phenomena. Man is the most perfect of organized beings. The moral and social world are also explained by this tendency to universal expansion, and the repression which results from the mutual action of all individuals upon each. It is needless to follow the details of these explanations. It is enough to state its conclusions in regard to the mind: the soul is a composite whole; the mind is a body, ideas are corpuscles; thought has extension, form, etc.

THEOLOGICAL SPIRITUALISM.

IT has been already stated that the reaction against sensualism was strengthened by the influence of many writers in the interest of religion and the Church. The most remarkable of these date from about the period of the restoration. While Royer-Collard and his disciples combated sensualism, and endeavoured to establish a contrary system by the philosophical observation of consciousness, the writers of the theological school confined all speculation within the limits of theological authority, and considered its only function to be that of explaining and justifying the doctrines received on the ground of Catholic faith. Negatively they bitterly opposed the doctrines of the sensual school, and wielded against them with great force the weapons of dialectics, invective, and ridicule.

Among these writers may be named CHATEAUBRIAND. Though a writer of imagination and sentiment rather than a philosopher, yet his aversion to sensualism, and the spiritual and religious tone of his works, were in harmony with the more decidedly philosophical writers of the theological school.

DE MAISTRE.

COUNT JOSEPH DE MAISTRE (born in 1753 in Piedmont, died at Turin in 1821) was a statesman and diplomatist, as well as a man of letters and a philosopher. He was an enemy to liberal principles in religion, politics, and philosophy, and an advocate of the principles typified by the Holy Alliance. His principal works are *On the Pope* (1819), and *Soirées at St. Petersburgh* (1821). The latter work, which, by its popular form, and its talent and wit, exerted great influence, touches upon almost all the great problems of metaphysics, running through a series of closely connected ideas with the apparent ease and grace of unstudied conversation.

The principal topic of his writings, in a philosophical view, is the temporal government of Providence. He endeavours to explain and justify the spectacle of the world so full of calamities and miseries for the good. He maintains, 1. That the good and the bad are both subject to suffering here below, but the good less than the bad; 2. That the good man suffers not as good, but as a man; 3. That man suffers in consequence of original sin; 4. That there are two means of deliverance, prayer on our own part, and intercession and merits of the good availing for us.

The foundation of political authority in the will of God; the divine right of legitimate sovereigns; passive obedience; the authority of the Church in matters of faith, the supremacy of the pope, and the superiority of ecclesiastical over the temporal authority: these are some of the religious and political principles of De Maistre. The practical tendencies of his system are to asceticism and mysticism.

LA MENNAIS.

To the same school, as indirectly an opponent of the sensual philosophy in behalf of the Church, belongs the celebrated Abbé de LA MENNAIS, who was born in 1780. In his earlier writings he was an ultra monarchist, and supporter of the principles of absolutism. In religion he was in favour of a state establishment, though he held the doctrines called in

France *ultramontane*, denying the freedom of the Gallican Church, and asserting for the pope absolute authority in spiritual matters, and insisting upon the dutiful submission of all governments to God in the Church. Subsequently he abandoned the political views he had at first put forth, and became a powerful advocate of liberal principles. Bold and vigorous in his tone of thinking, brilliant and eloquent in his style, his various writings have attracted great attention, and some of them have exerted great influence, though for the most part the ideas which they present are not within the scope of this work. He engages in philosophical investigations only for the sake of establishing a criterion of truth independent of reason.

The principal points in his book on *Indifference in Religion* are: his skepticism in regard to the intellectual faculties; authority as the sole principle of belief; and the applications of this principle.

1. He denies the possibility of philosophical knowledge. The senses are deceptive; sentiment is equally uncertain; and reason, operating only upon data given in sensation and sentiment, is more to be distrusted than either. All the contradictions, conflicts, extravagances, and impieties which the history of philosophy exhibits, show that, if man is to have truth and certainty only on philosophical grounds, man must forever remain in doubt.

2. There is no resting-place for the human mind but in the principle of authority. Authority is the sole rule of judgment. In defect of this, our judgments must be erroneous, or at least doubtful. Authority, with La Mennais, means the testimony of a sufficient number of competent witnesses. We are to confide in those who know.

3. La Mennais applies his principle chiefly to the

religious history of man. There have been three forms of religions in the world: the Patriarchal, the Mosaic, and the Christian—all derived by revelation from God. These three are substantially one. All forms of paganism and false religions are corruptions of revealed religion. His views imply the possibility, if not the likelihood, of still other developments of religion in the progress of humanity.

It is scarcely necessary to offer any critical remarks on this system. Unless the author allows in man some ground of truth, some faculty of cognition, his scientific skepticism becomes absolute skepticism. How is man to know what is a sufficient number of competent witnesses to give to testimony the force of authority? How did the witnesses derive the truth? From others, and they again from others, till we come to God? Had the first witnesses any certain faculty of recognising the revelation not given to us? The denial of all trustworthiness to sensation, sentiment, and reason, would make it impossible to answer these questions so as to avoid universal skepticism.

BONALD.

Of a more philosophical cast of mind is the Viscount de Bonald, although he has philosophized only on religious and political subjects. He was born in 1762. In 1791 he belonged to the liberal constitutional party, and was president of the departmental administration of Aveyron. Subsequently he attached himself to the legitimatist party. In 1815 he was a member of the chamber of deputies; afterward a peer of France, and under Villele a censor of the press. As a writer he is artificial and obscure in his style, yet sometimes expressing himself with simplicity and eloquence.

Bonald rejects consciousness as the instrument of philosophical investigation. He takes his starting-point from a primitive language given to man at creation. This fact he seeks to establish by historical and by metaphysical considerations. He considers it a sufficient demonstration of the impossibility of the invention of language, and, consequently, the necessity of its being a primitive revelation, that a system of words could never be invented without thought, and that thought would be impossible without words.

From this fact Bonald deduces a demonstration of the existence of an intelligent first cause; but beyond this he has made but little use of his principle in explaining the human faculties and their relations to language. In his principal work, *Inquiries concerning the Primary Objects of Moral Knowledge*, he has discussed a great variety of questions, and argued with great force and eloquence against materialism and its moral consequences, but the arguments he employs have no dependance whatever upon the fact which he set out with proclaiming as the sole principle of science.

The object and result of Bonald's speculations is to establish the Church as the highest authority in matters of truth. Everything not conformed to the Bible, as interpreted by the Church, is error and delusion, whether in religion, metaphysics, morals, or politics.

To the same class of writers belong also Baron D'ECKSTEIN (born in Denmark in 1785, settled in France since 1815), and BALLANCHE (born in 1776). Their writings, however, offer nothing for special remark. They write in a pure and elevated, but, at the same time, somewhat mystical religious spirit. In common with the writers already noticed, they maintain the insufficiency of philosophy, and uphold the principle of catholic authority.

RATIONAL PSYCHOLOGISTS, OR ECLECTIC SCHOOL.

WE come now to trace the more strictly philosophical movement in opposition to sensualism. We begin with the physiologists Berard and Virey.

BERARD.

BERARD was born in 1793, and died in 1828. Contrary to Cabanis and Bichat, he maintained the existence of an immaterial principle distinct from the organization in and through which it manifests itself. This principle is a force or power which actuates all organized nature, vegetable and animal. Berard distinguishes between the vital principle as manifested in the vegetable and merely animal world and in man; maintaining, however, the existence in both cases of an immaterial principle. In man, the bodily organs, so far from being the efficient or productive source of our faculties, are only its external instruments. It is not the brain that thinks, nor the stomach that digests; it is the intellectual power that thinks in the brain, it is the digestive power that digests in the stomach. The brain and the stomach are the conditions of the manifestation of these forces, the theatre on which they act. So far is life from resulting from the organization, that the organization itself is formed, sustained, unfolded, and preserved by the concurrence of a vital principle totally different from matter. Organized matter and these immaterial forces are intimately united, and exert a mutual influence in manifold ways. In man the vital and the intellectual power are both united to the physical organization, and the relations become still more complicated. The facts are observable: the manner of their union and action is inexplicable. Nevertheless, nothing can render the facts of observation and consciousness admissible, nothing can satisfy reason, but the supposition of these spiritual forces as the principle of the phenomena of life: while, on the other hand, the theory of materialism is burdened with great difficulties. Berard shows, from various facts, that it is not so certain as has been generally held that the brain is even the sole condition of sensation.

"The soul," he concludes, therefore, "is one, indivisible, immaterial. United to a body, it can come into this union only as a spirit, and not according to the law which unites body to body. It is not in juxtaposition with the organs, it is not interposed; it is simply present to them; it there feels; it imparts and receives activity. It is linked in the exercise of its activity to certain physiological and vital conditions, without which it could not display its faculties; but it does not owe its faculties to them: it is a force, a power, working in harmony with other forces, which, likewise united to the organism, have yet their special functions and properties."—*Doctrine of the Relations of the Physical and Moral in Man*, Paris, 1823.

VIREY.

VIREY, in his treatise on Vital Power (1823), takes the same general ground. The active power which is displayed in the universe is not to be conceived as a property or as a result of matter; it is a principle by itself, pervading, informing, and actuating matter, and producing all the phenomena of nature. Man is not a compound of material particles, whose organic combination engenders all the vital functions, but a simple force which penetrates, animates, and disposes the organism, and there produces the phenomena of life. God is the creator of all these powers.

We pass now to the psychological and metaphysical writers.

KERATRY.

KERATRY (born in 1769) published an ontological work under the title of *Moral and Physiological Inductions*. In the beginning there existed nothing but the Absolute Being. He was intelligent; willed to create; penetrated the infinite void of non-being, the eternal ground of the possibility of matter and spirit: gave reality to them, in the innumerable different forms of combination with which the universe is filled. In our world there resulted three great species of beings, mineral, vegetable, and animal—mixed beings, which all exhibit the alliances of spirit (or force) and matter in different degrees. These beings subsist for a time, then die; then force and matter, before united, are dissolved, not, however, to return to nonentity, but to go into new combinations. Of the soul of man, in particular, such is the constitution, that at the beginning it is united to the body only that it may afterward be set free, and reappear in different relations, where, doubtless, it will have other organs, more delicate and more perfect than those it possesses here below. Such is his theory of the creation by God of the spiritual and material world; their terrestrial union; their restoration in another world.

These ideas are developed by analogies and descriptions of a poetical cast, and by physiological and physical considerations.

His moral principles partake of a refined selfishness, though elevated by their alliance with his belief in God, in immortality, and a future life. He makes moral obligation rest on the generous and benevolent satisfaction of virtue, the sentiment of well-being that accompanies it. He makes happiness exclusively the chief end of man, and therefore the principle of virtue, forgetting that man was made for goodness; and, if made for happiness, it is because happiness is the consequence, the token, and reward of goodness. He thus resolves virtue into a certain kind of utility, though widely different from the utility of Volney and the grosser utilitarians. In a similar way he explains the beautiful into a form of the useful.

MASSIAS.

Massias (born in 1764) published a number of philosophical works, in which he not only opposed the principles of materialism, but attempted to establish the foundations of philosophy more securely than in his view had before been done. His disquisitions relate to nearly all branches of philosophy. His *Relations of Man to Nature and of Nature to Man*, and his *Problem of the Mind*, are his principal works. His views do not appear to contain anything peculiar, except the pretension of having discovered a firm basis for philosophy in a fact overlooked, in his opinion, by other philosophers. To us it seems to be an attempt, so far as it amounts to anything, analogous to those of Malebranche and Cudworth, to imagine an explanation of the inexplicable fact of the mutual influence of mind and matter in the human organism. We will, however, give the author's own words: "It is impossible to conceive any modification of our own being without an organic action; an intelligent action, which causes or which perceives it; and a universal action, which gives law both to the organization and the intelligence, and maintains them in their form and character.

"If it is undeniably true that nature acts continually upon our organization, exciting and regulating its operations, and if, nevertheless, this intervention has hitherto been made no account of, but man has always been considered apart from this primitive element of his being, it follows that no philosophy has yet been able to solve the problem of the mind, and lay the sure foundations of human knowledge. . . . This relation, this third element of the constitution of man, of which no account has hitherto been made, forms a TERNARY UNITY, having in itself the *cause* of its action, and, consequently, the *means* and the *effect;* and out of itself, consequently, its object, its stimulus, and its regulative principle, which, in perception, it associates with its action. . . . Man is thus a finite creature, dependant in his organization and his thinking upon the universe, and the laws which govern the universe, to the action of which he associates himself by perception and intelligence, and, in respect to his free-will, subject to the law of duty, which he can obey or disobey."

DEGERANDO.

DEGERANDO, in his earlier works, was a follower of Condillac, but subsequently abandoned his system, and attached himself to the spirit of the philosophy introduced by Royer-Collard and Cousin. He has not written any systematic works; but his book on Moral Improvement, and his Comparative History of Philosophy, are pervaded by an elevated and spiritual tone of thinking, and have been much esteemed.

LAROMIGUIERE.

LAROMIGUIERE has been mentioned as having given a special direction to the philosophical movement in France. He was a writer of eminent abilities, imbued with the true philosophical spirit; simple, lively, and acute in thinking; clear, easy, and graceful in style; expressing his ideas with equal elegance and precision. He was generally ranked among the disciples of Condillac; yet he introduced many important modifications, combating the sensual system on some points, and abandoning it on others. In regard to the faculties of the human mind, he does not follow Condillac either in the order of their development, or the number and systematic relation of them. But one of the most important points in which he departs from his master is in respect to the explanation which he gives of the principle of the faculties. Instead of seeking for the germe of them in the sensitive passivity, in sensation, he finds it in an opposite element, in the activity. Condillac supposes the soul altogether passive; Laromiguière believes it to be likewise active, and makes this activity an absolutely essential condition of its development.

So, also, he differs materially from Condillac on the question of the origin of ideas. With Condillac they are all derived from sensation alone as their origin and cause. Laromiguière distinguishes between the origin and matter of ideas, and the instrument and means of their production; between the *matter* of ideas or perceptions, and the *form* of them: the former he admits to be derived from sensation, but the latter is given by the intellectual activity. To experience a sensation is not in itself to think: this is a function of the intellectual activity. This activity is therefore admitted as an original attribute of the mind, and a co-ordinate source of knowledge. This view is contrary to the system of Condillac, and comes much nearer to the doctrine of Reid and Kant.

As to the rest, his analysis and classification of the faculties of the human mind is liable to many objections, which were brought forward by De Biran and others. His lectures, however, exerted a very salutary influence in weakening the exclusive control of sensualism; and were better adapted to this end, from the fact of their coming from a disciple of Condillac, and in the form they took, than if they had been in open, thorough, and consistent opposition.

DE BIRAN.

MAINE DE BIRAN (born in 1766, died in 1824) was originally a disciple of Cabanis and De Tracy, but afterward abandoned their system, and, in his Examination of the Lectures of Laromiguière, maintained that the soul is a cause, a power, an active principle: a view which he carries out to the exclusion of almost every other. He afterward maintained a modified form of the system of Leibnitz: an absolute spiritualism, which explains God, man, and the world, their essence and relations, by active principles and their activities. He adopted the monadism of Leibnitz, all but its doctrines of pre-established harmony and fatal predestination. He sets out from the observation of consciousness. This reveals the soul as an active force: active in all the modifications of the mind. External objects are only forces; consciousness recognises them only as causes of certain impressions; their different properties are different modes of their action. Minerals, vegetables, animals, all bodies, all beings in nature, are only forces or combinations of forces: active substances and their various actions. All forces are not, like the soul, intelligent and free, but all are more or less endowed with activity; even resistance, that most passive quality of matter, as it is commonly considered, is but a mode of activity. There are, therefore, not two sorts of substances in the world, forces and particles, but only forces; extension, form, etc., are only the impression produced by the active elements, whose property or mode of action is resistance. Matter is, accordingly, the continuity and co-existence of resisting forces producing a certain impression. Matter, therefore, is not denied any more than spirit; only their substantial difference is denied; both are explained in the same way; both are forces.

To explain the relations which exist between the soul and the body on these principles, becomes, in the view of De Biran, an easy thing. It is no longer necessary to inquire how a simple and active substance, and an inert and compound substance, can act and react upon each other; no need of imagining a mediator, half spirit, half matter: a contradictory notion, and useless besides; no need of the hypothesis of occasional causes or of pre-established harmony, which suppress the fact instead of explaining it; and, finally, no need of taking refuge in our ignorance, and bowing down to a mystery. We have only to reflect that the relations of body and soul are only relations of forces, of action and reaction. These forces, according to their peculiar degrees and modes of activity, appear now active, now passive; they are some of them the body, and some of them the mind.

The Creation is a composition of forces; the Creator is himself a force, an active principle; infinite, eternal, all-pervading; possessed of the plenitude of intelligence, goodness, bliss, will, and power.—Such is De Biran's doctrine of immaterialism. We shall make no other remark upon it than that the question of adopting or rejecting it turns entirely upon the question whether, in the analysis of consciousness, we find: 1. Sensations or impressions; 2. The reference of them to a cause or force; 3. An inert passive substance, in which the force resides, or with which it is connected.—The common sense of mankind believes the latter.

ROYER-COLLARD.

Peter Paul Royer-Collard was born about the year 1768. Before the revolution he was an advocate in the Parliament of Paris. During the revolution he was for a long time member of the Communal Council and of the Council of Five Hundred His moderation, and his hatred of anarchy and blood shed, subjected him to persecution during the Reign of Terror, and he withdrew into retirement, and devoted himself to philosophical studies. In 1811 he became dean of the Faculty of Letters at the Normal School, where he lectured with great applause. Subsequently, in 1814, he returned to public life; was president of the Council of Public Instruction, and when removed from that office on account of his liberal principles, was chosen a member of the Chamber of Deputies, of which body he became president. He was at the head of the political party of the *Doctrinaires*, who opposed the movements both of the ultra-liberal and of the royalist parties.

This celebrated man is entitled to an eminent place in the history of philosophy, less as a philosopher than as a professor. He was not the founder of a new system, but the eloquent and able expounder of the philosophy of Reid, and the successful opponent of the sensual system, which, up to the time when he began his lectures in 1811, was the ruling philosophy. The task he undertook required eminent personal qualities, and they were combined in him: a mind singularly vigorous, profound, and clear; ease, precision, and force of language; richness of imagination, and great eloquence. The influence he exerted was prodigious; it wrought a complete revolution in the philosophy of France. Of his philosophical labours, nothing exists in print but fragments of his lectures, published with explanations by his pupil Jouffroy, in connexion with the works of Reid.

In opposing the doctrines of Condillac and the sensual school, Royer-Collard rested chiefly upon the doctrines of Reid, whose system he expounded and enforced with great ability, though he has modified it in some respects by the manner and form of his applications, developed it more fully on some points, and added some special analyses of his own, particularly in regard to the theory of perception.

Directing against Condillac the objections urged by Reid against the doctrine of Locke, Berkeley, and Hume, he shows that, by the system which resolves all mental phenomena into sensation, we can have no knowledge of the existence of an external world. All we know are certain states of our own mind in sensation: we call them properties of an external substance, of matter existing out of the mind. But how do we know that there is any such substance really existing? By the sensual system we cannot know it; for it is in itself not a matter of sensation. We must even pronounce that it does not exist; for sensation is all the existence there is for us.

Royer-Collard then explains his view of the manner in which we attain the knowledge of the existence of the external world. It is in virtue of a fact of consciousness which he calls *natural induction*. It is not a reflective process, like scientific induction, but a spontaneous and necessary action of the mind which leads us to the idea and irresistible belief in the reality of the world without us. This fact is much insisted on, described and analyzed with great precision. It is at bottom, however, substantially one of Reid's principles of common sense, or Stewart's fundamental laws of human belief; and where Royer-Collard has gone farther than Reid in minute analysis, he has sometimes rendered himself liable to objections.

In like manner, he shows that the ideas of substance, cause, time, space, etc., cannot be explained on the principles of Condillac. They are not matters of sensation: they can in no way be resolved into any modification of it. So, likewise, of moral ideas.

Royer-Collard rendered important service to the progress of philosophy in France by his clear, original, and striking expositions of the method of observation and experiment in application to philosophy.

But the chief monuments of the powerful influence he exerted are his disciples and successors. He founded a school; he gathered around him a body of ardent and elevated young minds. To them he imparted his zeal, his spirit, his method, and his principles. In their labours we recognise the heart and mind of their master; while, at the same time, in conformity with the spirit which he inculcated, they have not rested in mere repetition of his particular views: if in some respects they have more fully developed and extended the doctrines of Royer-Collard, in others they have taken the course of free and independent inquiry. Among his disciples, the most celebrated is Cousin.

COUSIN.

VICTOR COUSIN, born in 1792, was educated at the Normal School, where he became an instructer in 1812. In 1815 he succeeded Royer-Collard as professor of philosophy in the Faculty of Letters in the University of Paris. He fell under the displeasure of government in 1820, and his lectures in the University were suspended; subsequently the Normal School was suppressed. On the fall of the administration of Villele in 1827, he was restored to his chair, and commenced a course of lectures, which was continued with brilliant success till 1830. He was then made member of the Council of Public Instruction, and principal of the Normal School, which he reorganized. In 1831 he went to Germany, under a special commission from government to examine the state of public instruction in that country. His reports have excited much attention. In 1832 he was made a peer of France, and in 1840 minister of public instruction.

In philosophy, Cousin acknowledges his obligations to Laromiguière and to De Biran, by whom his mind was put in a direction contrary to the prevailing sensualism; but more especially to Royer-Collard, whose pupil and disciple he was before he became his successor. In his earliest instructions he confined himself chiefly to expounding the ideas of his master. He soon, however, extended his researches into every sphere of philosophical inquiry, particularly the critical history of philosophy, both ancient and modern; until at length he formed a system of his own, which has received the denomination of Eclecticism.

This system has not been developed at large in any one complete and systematic work; but all the leading principles of it, with their systematic connexion and their applications, may be gathered from the author's various writings. A brief summary will be attempted.

Exposition.

The principal points to which everything in this system may be referred, are: its method; application of its method to psychology; passage from psychology to ontology; general views on the history of philosophy.

I. *Method.*

There is nothing peculiar in the principle of his method; it is the method of induction, which has been everywhere proclaimed in the philosophy of the eighteenth century. It is the same method applied to the phenomena of the mind, as in physical science is applied to the phenomena of nature. Philosophy, equally with physics, is a science of facts. In physics these facts are given by the senses, in philosophy by consciousness. In both cases the application of the method of induction is substantially the same, and governed by the same general rules. In the first place, a careful and complete *observation* of facts; in the second place, *experiment* and *reasoning* applied to the facts observed. In philosophy no less than in physics, mere observation of facts is barren, and leads to no results. It is not sufficient merely to listen to nature, we must interrogate it; it is not enough to observe, we must experiment. In philosophy, reflection is the instrument of experiment, and is analogous to the artificial instruments and reproductive processes of physical experiment.—So much for method in general.

In regard to method in particular, Cousin makes psychology the basis and starting-point of all true philosophy. Psychology is the observation and classification of the phenomena of the mind. These phenomena must be accurately observed; none omitted; none supposed. They must be observed in simplicity and good faith. If neglected, or if observed with any systematic bias, psychology, and with it all philosophy, are corrupted at the source: we fall inevitably into hypotheses.

The true method was proclaimed by Descartes, by Locke and his followers; but it was almost immediately corrupted in its application by systematic views. They looked only for such facts as suited their preconceived conceptions; hence facts were partially observed and distorted; observation, experiment, and induction were vitiated from the beginning. They fell into hypothesis.

On the other hand, the new German philosophy has repudiated the psychological method. It begins with the absolute, and comes to psychology by metaphysics and physics combined. Now, even although ontology contain the root of psychology, it can never be known until verified by psychological observation; and to set out from it is to enter upon the hazardous path of hypothesis. It is to make philosophy, not an *inductive*, but a *constructive* science. Building thus the structure from the top downward, we are liable to substitute for facts arbitrary abstractions and the caprices of the imagination. The new German philosophy has committed a serious error in point of method. The psychological method is the true method; psychology is not the whole of philosophy, but it is its foundation.

II. *Application of Method to Psychology.*

Cousin divides all the phenomena of consciousness into three classes, referable to three great elementary faculties, which in their combinations comprise and explain all others. These faculties are sensibility, activity, and reason. These three faculties enter simultaneously into exercise, and are blended together in the unity of consciousness: but, however inseparable they may be in the unity of the intellectual life, they are yet perfectly distinct.

Sensible and rational facts have one characteristic

in common, which distinguishes them from voluntary facts: they are both independent of the control of the will; that is to say, we do not impute sensations and judgments of reason to ourselves as the products of our own voluntary activity. When the conditions of a sensation or a rational idea are accomplished, our will cannot prevent the sensibility or the reason from entering into exercise. The sensation or the idea become facts of consciousness necessarily, in spite of the will.

The activity alone is marked with the characteristics of personality and responsibility. The will is the constituent element of personality. It is only in the activity of the will that we are able to recognise ourselves, to say *me;* yet it is only by distinguishing ourselves from our sensations and their objects that we can have self-consciousness; and, as we cannot perceive ourselves, and distinguish ourselves from our sensations, except by a faculty of perception in general, it follows that the exercise of reason is contemporaneous with the exercise of personal activity and with sensible impressions. The essential element of cognition is reason; and consciousness, though composed of three integrant and inseparable elements, has its most immediate foundation in reason, without which there would be no possible knowledge, and, consequently, no consciousness. Reason is thus intimately connected with personality and with sensibility, but it is neither the one nor the other. Sensibility is the external condition of consciousness; the will is its centre, and reason is its light.

Of the Sensibility a more particular psychological analysis is not necessary here, as there is nothing in the system of Cousin which particularly distinguishes it from other systems in relation to the organs of sensation, and the classification of their various affections with respect to the corresponding qualities of external objects.

The WILL is the element of personality and causality. Our notion of cause is first apprehended by the reason in the consciousness of our own personal activity. The movements of the sensibility, desires, passions, etc., so far from constituting the will, are entirely distinct from it, and may stand in direct opposition to it. The will is in its essence a cause, a power, a force. The internal causal energy of the will must not be confounded with any of its instruments or external manifestations. We do not find the primitive notion of cause in the action of the will on our nervous and muscular organization, and much less in the force communicated by the muscles to external objects. A perfect paralysis of the muscles could not prevent the internal act of the will. The primitive notion of personal cause, to wit, our own will, becomes the type and condition of the notion of cause in general, and of external impersonal causes.

There is a twofold activity of the will, spontaneous and reflective. The spontaneous is the primitive form, the reflective is the ulterior. The fact of the former is necessarily presupposed in the latter; we cannot reflect upon what has not existed in a spontaneous form. These two forms of activity are distinguished by Cousin by the terms spontaneous and voluntary, or spontaneity and will, appropriating the terms voluntary, and activity, and will to the reflective form of activity.

All personal acts, whether spontaneous or voluntary, have their cause in an active power; the activ ity is itself the only cause of all particular actions;

in this consists the essence of freedom. The very notion of liberty is that of a power which acts by an energy within itself—a power of self-determination. Liberty is not self-determination in act, but self-determination in power, which in act, in volitions, determines itself in this or that particular form.

In the REASON or intelligence analysis discovers three integrant elements or laws of thought, which both constitute it and govern its activity: 1. The idea of *infinite* (expressed likewise indifferently by the terms unity, substance, absolute cause, the absolute, etc.); 2. The idea of the *finite* (expressed likewise by the terms plurality, phenomenon, relative cause, the conditioned, etc.); 3. The idea of the *relation* between the infinite and finite: a relation not simply of inseparable coexistence, but of cause and effect.

These three elements are given inseparably in the primitive synthesis of thought. They constitute the unity of reason, which is manifested in this triple action.

Reason, which manifests itself in these three ideas, is not individual or personal. It is not a part of our free activity. Reason is constituted and governed by these absolute and necessary conceptions. It is therefore absolute in its essence; it is one with the eternal and divine reason; it is relatively human only as manifesting itself in the phenomena of human consciousness. The necessary convictions of reason which we find in our consciousness cannot be conceived by us as merely relative to our minds or to the minds of our fellow-men. They appear as universal truths, truths for all intelligences, truths to the divine intelligence equally as to us, but no more than to us; that is, they are truths in themselves, truths absolute; truths which we can neither make, deny, nor modify by an act of our own will; which no will in the universe can make, deny, or modify. It is only when, by a voluntary act of reflection, we fall back upon them as phenomena of our own consciousness, and they thus become blended with what is individual and personal in our consciousness, that they have any appearance of being subjective and relative to our personality. In itself and its action, reason is essentially impersonal.

All the absolute laws of thought or regulative principles of reason may be reduced to two: the law of causality, that every phenomenon supposes a cause; and the law of substance, that every quality supposes a substance. These two are the fundamental principles, of which all others are derivatives. They are given to us contemporaneously in the unity of consciousness; or, if they are to be distinguished, the law of substance is *logically* the first, and that of causality the second; the idea of substance, that is, being necessarily implied, as that without which there could be no idea of cause: but the law of causality is *chronologically* the first, and that of substance the second; the idea of cause, that is, must be first in the order of acquisition as the condition of the idea of substance.

In reducing the laws of thought fundamentally to these two, Cousin differs from preceding philosophers. Plato attempted no enumeration and classification. Aristotle gave a complete enumeration of them, but he did not reduce them to their fundamental elements; and, besides, his arrangement of them is arbitrary, and does not correspond to the development of intelligence. The Cartesians recognised necessary truths, but made no attempt at a complete and precise enumeration of them. The sensual school of the eighteenth century recognised none, and, of course, gave no classification. The Scottish school restored them to honour, but gave no complete account of them. Kant renewed the attempt of Aristotle, and was the first among the moderns who attempted a complete list of the laws of thought; but he is arbitrary in his classification, and his list is capable of reduction.

The development of reason is twofold. The constituent elements of reason are all found in consciousness. But how are they found? In the developed state of human intelligence we find them by reflection. The finite supposes the infinite, the infinite the finite: they are reciprocally correlatives. But these elements were not *originally* given in a reflective process of intelligence, in which an act of attention, of will, is blended with reason. Reflection only adds *itself* to what already was in the mind: it falls back upon, analyzes, distinguishes, throws clearer light upon, but does not create the elements to which it applies itself. Reflection therefore presupposes an anterior operation of the intelligence. As this operation is not of reflection, it does not imply the exercise of the voluntary activity or will. It is therefore an instinctive development of thought; and as intelligence does not begin by negation, this primitive operation is an instinctive perception of truth, an immediate intuition and a pure affirmation.

There is thus a twofold development of reason: the first primitive, unreflective, instinctive; the second ulterior, reflective, voluntary. The first is termed spontaneous reason, spontaneity of reason, or, briefly, spontaneity; the second reflective reason, reflection of reason, or, briefly, reflection.

III. *Passage from Psychology to Ontology.*

Ontology is the science of being. It has to do, not with mere subjective or phenomenal, but with objective or substantial existence. Its province is to answer the question: Whether anything exists beyond the sphere of our own consciousness, and whether we can have certain knowledge of it? Cousin maintains that we can proceed legitimately from the facts of consciousness to the knowledge of our own existence, of the world, and of God. And this knowledge he makes to be immediate, positive, and absolute. The principle of it he finds in the distinction between spontaneous and reflective reason. Reflective reason becomes subjective by the blending of an element of personality, an act of our own will, with the operation of reason in our consciousness; but reason in itself is impersonal, and in spontaneous reason there is nothing subjective: it is a pure apperception and absolute affirmation. It is immediate cognition, in which is given to us everything that subsequently, under a logical form and by means of reflection, becomes necessary truth.

The regular development of reason in consciousness takes us legitimately beyond the limits of consciousness, and attains to the knowledge of external or objective existence. We must either deny the authority of consciousness altogether, or admit its authority without reserve for the facts it attests, even though they transcend the sphere of our phenomenal states. The reason, in its development in consciousness, is no less certain and real than the sensibility and the will; its certainty once admitted, we must follow it when it conducts us from our own sphere to things existing out of ourselves.

For example, it is a rational fact attested by consciousness, that, in the view of intelligence, every phenomenon which is presented supposes a cause. It is a fact, moreover, that this principle of causality is marked with the characteristics of universality and necessity. If it be universal and necessary, to limit it would be to destroy it. Now, in the phenomenon of sensation, the principle of causality intervenes universally and necessarily, and refers this phenomenon to a cause; and our consciousness testifying that this cause is not the personal cause which the will represents, it follows that the principle of causality conducts us to an impersonal cause, to an external cause: the aggregate of such causes, generalized as laws, make up the outward world, nature, or the universe. Here, then, is objective existence, but existence revealed by a principle which is attested by consciousness. Here is a primary step in ontology, but by the path of psychology, that is, of internal observation.

In a similar way we are led to the Cause of all causes, to the substantial Cause, to God; and not only to a God of Power, but to a God of Justice, a God of Holiness.

The laws of thought thus being demonstrated to be absolute, induction can make use of them without hesitation; and from absolute principles, obtained by observation, can legitimately conduct us to a point beyond the immediate sphere of observation itself. The two fundamental laws of thought, as has been said, are the law of causality and the law of substance.

Applied to the phenomena of our own personal activity, they give us the knowledge of our own substantial and causal existence.

Applied to our sensations, which we cannot refer to ourselves as their cause, they give us the external world, nature, in the character of the cause of the phenomena we experience.

Thus we have the knowledge of the me and of the not-me. These are both given in consciousness as limited or finite.

But it is equally a fact of observation that reason does not stop with the finite. As soon as the notion of the finite is given, we cannot but conceive the infinite. With every notion of finite cause and substance is immediately and necessarily connected the notion of infinite cause and substance, that is, of God, and of the relation of the finite to the infinite.

Such as a psychological fact is the necessary development of reason in consciousness. In this triplicity the unity of consciousness unfolds itself. This we now recognise by reflection; but this process has all taken place in the spontaneous reason, and therein gave us immediate and positive cognition before we reflected on it; and it still and always gives knowledge to such as may, perhaps, never reflect upon it. In the spontaneous operation of reason mankind instinctively distinguish between their thoughts and volitions, and the substance and subject of them, calling the latter me; instinctively, also, they recognise the relation between thoughts and volitions and themselves, referring the former to the latter, as attribute to substance, and effect to cause. They may never express this in terms; they may never reflect upon it; or they may not possess the power of reflection and expression sufficiently to state it; but none the less does the process take place. It is the universal process, the same in all minds, the peasant and the philosopher; only the philosopher reflects, analyzes, abstracts, and expresses the process in logical formulas or with scientific precision.

So, likewise, the spontaneous reason distinguishes

between sensations and their external causes, and instinctively recognises the outward world as the substance and cause of all the qualities and phenomena which the mind observes in sensation.

So, again, the spontaneous reason, immediately that it recognises the me and the not-me, self and the world, as finite, instinctively recognises the infinite cause and substance to which everything finite must be referred. The finite and the infinite are correlatives in knowledge; the former cannot be regarded as a matter of positive cognition any more than the latter. If we deny the latter as an object of positive cognition, we must likewise deny the former; for they have both the same title; both are given inseparably in the unity of consciousness.

Psychology thus contains and reflects all knowledge, God and nature no less than man.

God is the absolute substance and cause; absolute intelligence, will, and goodness. The divine intelligence is likewise a triplicity in unity.

Creation is comprehensible and necessary; that is to say, it is the manifestation of the infinite in the finite, of unity in variety. God, as absolute substance and absolute cause, is the absolute One. But, as absolute cause, *we* cannot but *conceive* that God should act; it is repugnant to reason to conceive that the absolute cause should forever remain inactive. But we cannot conceive the absolute cause to act otherwise than by determining itself; that is to say, we cannot conceive the infinite to manifest itself actively but in the finite, the unity in variety. For God to act, then, is to create; and creation, at least relatively to our mental constitution, is the necessary manifestation of the divine activity.

God is not, however, to be confounded with the creation; nor is God a mere soul of the world. God is the cause, the universe is the effect. While the universe, both of intelligent and unintelligent beings, is the necessary manifestation of the creative activity of God, the Creator still remains in his absolute divine essence and personality, distinct from, and unexhausted by, the creation, and retaining all the superiority of cause to the effect, of infinite cause to the (necessarily) finite effect. While, therefore, the creation is a manifestation and reflection of God, it is a limited, and, therefore, necessarily imperfect reflection of him.

Psychology also contains the principles of all true Physics. Two laws, and their connexion in perpetual reaction, govern and explain the material world. These two laws are expansion and attraction. External nature is conceived as an assemblage of forces, governed by these two laws; the various phenomena of nature are results of the reciprocal action of these laws, and of the multiform determinations of these forces.

In Morals, Cousin strenuously maintains, as the only possible condition of a moral law, that freedom of the will which he had also psychologically demonstrated as a fact. The moral law can command only a free will. The Infinite and Eternal Will is revealed to us in conscience in the supreme law: "Will what is good;" and the human individual unites with the Infinite Will only in freely obeying its voice.

Repudiating also the doctrine of the exclusive origin of our ideas in sensation, and demonstrating that our ideas of right and wrong, and of duty, can never be found in sensation, nor in consciousness except as revealed there by reason, he earnestly opposes every form of the selfish system by which virtue is resolvec into utility, and self-interest made the ground of obligation and the motive of action.

He also opposes all moral systems grounded upon sympathy or benevolence, or any other sentiment, considered as mere sentiments or emotions. Mere emotion is variable and contingent, not in itself the subject of moral law; and, even if erected into a principle of obligation, would not suffice to explain all moral facts, or constitute a system.

The general principles of the morality of self-interest are variable and contingent principles, and, if erected into an exclusive system, are destructive of the absolute moral principles revealed in the reason.

The fundamental maxim of the morality of self-interest in regard to an action to be performed is: Look only at its consequences relative to personal happiness.

The most important general maxims resulting from this are:

Do right, abstain from wrong, from hope or fear of the rewards and penalties of civil society;

Do right, abstain from wrong, from hope or fear of divine rewards or punishments;

Do right, abstain from wrong, from fear of blame from others, and even of remorse, and in order to gain the pleasure of a good conscience and internal happiness.

These contingent principles of self-interest or prudence have a legitimate sphere of influence in subordination to the absolute principles of the moral law, and only in such subordination. But there is an absolute, essential, and immutable difference between right and wrong. Right and wrong are absolute and ultimate conceptions of the reason; all actions, conceivable as well as real, in all times and places, are necessarily and universally qualified by reason, according to these conceptions, as right or wrong in themselves, or else they are morally indifferent. Hence necessary moral principles.

The conceptions of right and wrong necessarily and immediately awaken the idea of obligation, the moral law.

The fundamental principle of obligation, or enunciation of the moral law, is: Do right for the sake of right; or, rather, Will the right for the sake of right.

The criterion by which an act or resolution may be recognised as conformed to this principle, is the impossibility of not considering the immediate motive of the particular act or resolution as universally binding.

With the conception of right and wrong is connected not only the absolute conviction of obligation, but also of merit and demerit; a principle not to be confounded with the moral law, nor with the instinctive desire for happiness.

The question of the sovereign good cannot be resolved by a single element. The Epicureans make it the satisfaction of the desire for happiness; the Stoics make it the fulfilment of the moral law. The true solution is in the harmony of both, not as equivalent principles, but in virtue as the antecedent of happiness. In this connexion the sovereign good is constituted of both; but of the two, virtue is the chief good.

In Æsthetics, Cousin maintains the idea of the Beautiful, as also an absolute conception of the reason, and, like other absolute ideas, having an absolute object existing independently of our necessary conception. This idea he distinguishes from every form of the agreeable or useful, and upon it builds a corresponding system of Æsthetics, or theory of the arts and criticism of the productions of the creative imagination.

IV. *Application of Rational Psychology to the History of Philosophy.*

It is in relation to the views which it takes of the history of philosophy that Cousin denominates his system eclecticism. Eclecticism is a method rather than a system: it is the method by which a system is applied to the criticism of all other systems, on the ground that a truly complete and correct system will explain the whole history of philosophy, and will be itself justified by the history of philosophy. For all the great systems that have appeared in history, however subversive of each other, contain each some portion of truth, and, consequently, some things in common with the comprehensive system by which they are judged. Eclecticism is therefore a method both philosophical and historical. Rational psychology at once explains and is verified by the history of philosophy. Three things are accordingly to be distinguished in eclecticism: its starting-point, its processes, and its end; or, in other words, its principle, its instruments, and its results. It supposes a system as its starting-point and clew through the labyrinth of history; its instrument is a rigid criticism, sustained on solid and extensive erudition; its primary result is the decomposition of all systems; and its final result the reconstruction from their materials of a new system, which shall be a complete representation of consciousness in history, and, at the same time, correspond to the results of rational psychology.

The application of this eclectic method discloses, as a matter of fact in the history of philosophy, four great systems, which comprehend all the attempts of the philosophical spirit, and which are found in every great philosophical epoch. These systems are sensualism, idealism, skepticism, and mysticism.

Sensualism takes sensation as the sole principle of knowledge. Sensation, indeed, is the principle of a large share of our knowledge, but not of the whole. Sensualism has therefore an element of truth: its error is in its exclusive pretension of explaining all knowledge by sensation. Its consequences are materialism, fatalism, and atheism.

Idealism, on the other hand, makes the intelligence or the ideas, which are the laws of reason, the sole principle of knowledge. An important part of our knowledge has, indeed, its origin in reason, but not all; and idealism, by erecting a partial truth into a universal one, finds all reality in the mind, denies matter, and absorbs all things, God and the universe, into individual consciousness, and that into thought.

Skepticism, disgusted with the extravagances of the two exclusive systems, easily demonstrates the error that there is in both; but not distinguishing the part of truth and the part of error that there is in both, it falls likewise into exclusiveness, declares every system false, and finally, with equal extravagance, declares that there is no such thing as certainty, thus falling into the absurd and suicidal dogmatism: it is certain that there is no certainty.

Mysticism is not the despair of philosophy and the renunciation of reflection to take refuge in religious authority, though this is a state of mind not infrequent; but it is reflection itself, grounding a system on an element of consciousness overlooked by sensualism, by idealism, and by skepticism—the element of spontaneity, which is the basis of reflection, reason, namely, referred to its eternal principle, and speaking with his authority in the human intelligence. But this system, overlooking the other elements of human nature, engenders multiplied extravagances, such as were displayed in the Alexandrian school, and have been displayed in every age.

These four systems contain all the fundamental elements of philosophy, and, consequently, of the history of philosophy. They have each their part of truth, which it is the business of eclecticism to distinguish from their part of error, and to combine together into the unity and harmony of a comprehensive system.

Observations.

1. In adopting the method of internal observation, and making psychology the basis of all philosophy, Cousin agrees with Locke and the sensual school, with the Scottish school, and with Kant, and differs from Schelling and the new German philosophy.

But he refuses to limit philosophy within the sphere of psychology, and contends for a philosophy of the absolute and infinite. In this respect he differs from Locke, Reid, and Kant, and agrees with Schelling and the later Germans.

But while he agrees with Schelling in making the absolute and infinite a positive in knowledge, he differs fundamentally from him in the mode of attaining it. Cousin finds it in consciousness; Schelling in a faculty transcending consciousness: Cousin in the spontaneous reason; Schelling in Intellectual Intuition, which, being a faculty out of consciousness, is a pure hypothesis.

It will be seen, therefore, that the peculiarity of the system of Cousin consists not merely in making the absolute and infinite a matter of positive cognition, but in holding the twofold distinction of reason into spontaneous and reflective, and in making the former, as impersonal, and, therefore, not subjective, the faculty of immediately knowing the absolute and infinite. The spontaneous reason apprehends the absolute and infinite by an act of positive knowledge; it reveals them in consciousness, but without thereby making them merely subjective.

It is, indeed, the great problem of speculative inquiry, whether there can be any objective knowledge of the unconditioned, or, in other words, whether philosophy is possible, considered as anything more than the observation and analysis of the *phenomena* of consciousness. The objective reality of the infinite and absolute may, however, be admitted on either ground. Reid and Kant admit the existence of God on the ground of the necessary convictions of the reason (we need not here advert to the differences in their modes of arriving at their result); Schelling and Cousin admit the Divine existence on the ground of positive knowledge. The former attain to God by Faith, the latter by Cognition. In a practical point of view, it may be thought to come to the unimportant verbal question whether our conviction of the Divine existence be a belief or a knowledge. But in speculation the difference is material.

2. The system of Cousin has been accused of pantheism. This charge is denied by the author. Pantheism is certainly not expressed anywhere in his writings, but the reverse; nor is there anything in his principles from which it becomes a necessary consequence, taking the word either in its proper or improper sense. He neither (in the proper sense of the word pantheism) confounds the infinite with the finite, making God to be nothing but the collective Whole of the universe, nor (in the improper sense of the word) confounds the finite with the infinite, denying, that is, the substantial existence of the finite,

and making the Infinite One the only Being. Spinoza and the Eleatics make God the sole substance, and a mere substance, of which all finite particular beings are merely attributes or qualities. Cousin represents God, not only as the absolute substance, but also as the absolute cause, free, personal, and intelligent, and perfectly distinct from finite beings, which are his creatures. The Infinite One is neither identified with the Whole, nor is the distinct substantial existence of the world, the substantial and personal existence of man, absorbed into the Absolute Unity. On the one hand, the collective Whole of all things does not constitute God; nor, on the other, is the collective Whole merely modes of God, the One and Sole Being. He neither makes the All the only Being, nor God the only Being.

3. The system of Cousin, from what has been seen in the exposition, must not be confounded with the Alexandrian doctrines, as perhaps the term eclecticism might at first lead one to imagine. That system, though professing the principle of eclecticism, belongs to the class denominated by Cousin mystical. Neither, as will be obvious from what has been said in the foregoing pages, is it the absence of system. Eclecticism is a system, or, rather, it supposes a system, sets out from a system, and applies a system. It takes a system as the criterion of the truth or falsehood of the systems it judges. Nor is it the mixture of all systems. It is the very opposite of syncretism. It does not mix; it chooses out: it does not confuse; it discriminates.

NOTE.

Disciples of Cousin.—Jouffroy.

Cousin has gathered around him numerous disciples, several of whom have already distinguished themselves in the cultivation of philosophy. Among these are Damiron, Jouffroy, Garnier, Vacherot.

Of these, the most distinguished is THEODORE JOUFFROY, born in 1796, and now professor of philosophy in the Faculty of Literature in Paris. He is the translator of Stewart's Outlines of Moral Philosophy, which he accompanied with a valuable preface; also of Reid's Works, with which he connected the Fragments of Royer-Collard's Lectures. Though adopting the general conclusions of Cousin, he is no mere repeater of his ideas, but exhibits eminent abilities as an original scientific observer; his modes of thinking and developments are entirely his own.

He has especially devoted himself to illustrating and establishing the general principles of the true psychological method of observation, and to morals. The great question, in his view, which lies at the bottom of all genuine philosophical inquiries, is that which concerns the nature and the destiny of man; two distinct points, yet never to be separated. This view constitutes the unity of his philosophical labours, which have been devoted to the progressive development of his ideas on this question. Of the lectures he has given in this course, a portion, under the title of *Introduction to Ethics*, has been published, which contains a critical review of the various systems that have prevailed in relation to the fundamental principles of morality. Another volume, containing the full exposition of his own systematic views, is to complete this Introduction; and this is to be followed by four other works on the different branches of ethics.

Of this course it is not time to speak; only it is but just to remark of the portion already published, that it is a production of the very highest ability, characterized by a scrupulous adherence to the methods of psychological observation, by the greatest depth and accuracy of thought, united with a transparent clearness of method and style. It proclaims and vindicates the absolute and immutable distinction of right and wrong, the absolute law of moral obligation, and the idea of right in itself as the motive of moral action.

CHRONOLOGICAL TABLE

OF THE

STORY OF PHILOSOPHY

FROM THE TIME OF THALES.

B.C.	
640	Thales born, according to Apollodorus.
630	Solon born.
629	Thales born, according to Meiners.
611	Anaximander born.
608	Pythagoras born, according to Larcher.
598	Solon publishes his laws. Pherecydes born about this time.
597	Thales prodicts an eclipse.
584	Pythagoras born, according to Meiners.
561	Solon died.
557	Anaximenes flourished.
548	Thales died.
547	Anaximander died.
543	Thales died, according to some. Pherecydes died.
540	Pythagoras founds a school at Crotona.
536	Xenophanes at Elea.
504	Pythagoras died. Parmenides flourished, according to some.
500	Anaxagoras and Philolaus born. Heraclitus and Leucippus flourished.
	Anaximenes died.
496	Ocellus Lucanus flourished.
494	Democritus born.
490	Battle of Marathon.
489	Pythagoras died, according to some.
480	Battle of Salamis.
472	Diogenes of Apollonia flourished.
470	Democritus born, according to Thrasyllus.
469	SOCRATES born. Parmenides flourished.
460	Parmenides comes from Elea to Athens with Zeno.
	Archelaus flourished. Democritus born, according to Apollodorus.
	Empedocles flourished, according to some.
456	Anaxagoras comes to Athens.
450	Xenophon born.

B.C.	
444	Melissus.
	Gorgias writes his treatise *Of Nature.*
442	Protagoras—Prodicus flourished.
432	Beginning of the Peloponnesian War.
431	Anaxagoras accused of impiety.
430	Plato born, according to Corsini.
428	Anaxagoras died.
427	Gorgias sent to Athens. Diagoras flourished.
414	Diogenes of Sinope born.
407	Democritus died, according to Eusebius.
404	End of the Peloponnesian War.
400	SOCRATES died. His disciples withdraw to Megara. Euclid flourished.
389	First voyage of Plato to Syracuse.
384	Aristotle born. Pyrrho born.
380	Antisthenes and Aristippus flourished.
	Aristotle goes to Athens.
	Eudoxus the Pythagorean flourished.
364	Second voyage of Plato to Syracuse.
361	Third Voyage of Plato to Syracuse.
360	Xenophon died.
356	Alexander born.
348	Plato died. Speusippus succeeds him.
347	Aristotle attaches himself to Hermias.
343	Aristotle preceptor of Alexander.
340	Diogenes and Crates, Cynics. Pyrrho and Anaxarchus flourished. Zeno of Citium born.
339	Speusippus died. Xenocrates begins to teach.
337	Battle of Cheronea. Epicurus born.
336	Philip, king of Macedon, died. Alexander succeeds him.
335	Aristotle opens his school at the Lyceum.
324	Diogenes the Cynic died.
323	Alexander the Great died. Ptolemy Lagus in Egypt.
322	Aristotle died. Theophrastus succeeds him.
320	Demetrius Phalereus and Dicæarchus of Messina flourished
316	Arcesilaus died (or later).
314	Xenocrates died. Polemo succeeds him.
313	Theophrastus becomes celebrated. Crates.
305	Epicurus opens his school at Athens.
300	Stilpo and Theodorus the Atheist flourished.
	Zeno founds a school at Athens.
	Diodorus and Philo.
288	Pyrrho died. Strato succeeds him.
286	Theophrastus died.
285	Ptolemy Philadelphus king of Egypt.
280	Chrysippus born.
272	Timon flourished.
270	Epicurus died.
269	Strato died. Lycon succeeds him.
264	Zeno the Stoic died (or later). Cleanthes succeeds him.

B.C.	
260	Perseus. Aristo of Chios. Herillus flourished.
241	Arcesilaüs died (or later).
217	Carneades born.
212	Zeno of Tarsus flourished.
208	Chrysippus died, according to Menage. Diogenes of Babylon.
185	Panætius died (according to others, later).
155	Embassy of the Athenians to Rome (Critolaüs, Carneades the Stoic, and Diogenes of Babylon).
146	Greece and Carthage subdued by Rome.
	Antipater of Tarsus.
142	Macedonia a Roman province.
135	Posidonius born.
129	Carneades died. Clitomachus succeeds him.
115	Panætius accompanies Scipio Africanus to Alexandria
107	Cicero born (or, according to some, 106).
106	Clitomachus died. Succeeded by Philo.
	Posidonius flourished.
86	Sylla takes Athens. Philo flees to Rome.
	Antiochus.
84	Lucretius born (according to others, earlier).
69	Antiochus died.
63	Judea a Roman province.
50	Posidonius died. Succeeded by Jason.
	Lucretius died.
48	Cratippus the Peripatetic flourished.
44 or 43	Cicero died.
30	Egypt a Roman province.
27	Augustus emperor. Philo the Jew born.

A.D.	*Roman Emperors.*	
2	Augustus.	Seneca born.
		Sextius the Pythagorean.
		Nicholas of Damascus and Xenarchus flourished.
		Athenodorus the Stoic.
14	Tiberius.	
15		Sotion.
33		Death of our Lord.
34		Philo the Jew flourished
37	Caligula.	Flavius Josephus born.
41	Claudius.	
50		Plutarch of Cheronea born.
54	Nero.	
65		Seneca put to death.
66		Cornutus and Musonius exiled.

A.D.	*Roman Emperors.*	
69	Galba, Otho.	
	Vitellius.	Apollonius of Thyane flourished.
70	Vespasian.	Euphrates of Egypt.
79	Titus.	
81		Musonius recalled from exile.
82	Domitian.	Philosophers and mathematicians banished from Rome.
89		Justin Martyr born.
		Epictetus flourished.
90		Apollonius of Thyane died.
97	Nerva.	Plutarch flourished.
99	Trajan.	Tacitus.
		The Gnostics.
118	Hadrian.	Secundus of Athens. Plutarch died.
120		Euphrates died.
122		Galienus born. Phavorinus.
131		Basilides the Gnostic.
134		Arrian flourished.
138		The Rabbi Akhiba died.
139	Antoninus Pius.	Calvisius Taurus. Apollonius the Stoic.
		Basilides the Stoic.
		Apuleius.
161	Marcus Aurelius.	Alcinoüs. Numenius.
165		Peregrinus the Cynic died.
		Justin Martyr died.
		Lucian.
170		Athenagoras and Tatian.
		Atticus the Platonist.
		Bardesanes.
180	Commodus.	Maximus Tyrius.
		Sextus Empiricus.
		Irenæus.
		The Rabbi Juda. The Talmud.
185		Origen born.
193	Pertinax.	Ammonius Saccas founds a school.
	Salvius.	The New-Platonists.
	Julian.	Clement of Alexandria.
	Septimius Severus.	Alexander of Aphrodisia.
		Galienus died.
200 } 205 }		Plotinus born. Philostratus.
212	Caracalla.	Clement of Alexandria died. Succeeded in the school of Alexandria by Pantænus.
218	Marcrinus.	Tertullian died.
220	Heliogabalus.	
222	Alexander Severus.	
232		Plotinus becomes the disciple of Ammonius.

A.D.	*Roman Emperors.*	
233		Porphyry. Ulpian.
235	Maximin.	
238	Gordian.	
239	Gordian II.	
242		Plotinus travels in the East.
243		Plotinus comes to Rome.
244	Philip.	
246		Amelius disciple of Plotinus.
250	Trajan Decius.	
252	Trebonian.	
	Gallus and Vibius Hostilianus.	Longinus flourished.
253	Æmilius Valerian.	Origen died.
269	Flavius Claudius.	
270	Aurelian.	Plotinus died.
275		Longinus put to death.
276	Tacitus.	
277	Probus.	*Manicheism.*
282	Aurelius Carus.	
284	Diocletian.	Arnobius.
304	Constantine and Maximin.	Porphyry died.
306	Constantine.	
321	Constantine becomes a Christian.	Iamblichus flourished. Lactantius flourished.
326		Arnobius died. Lactantius died.
333		Iamblichus died. Themistius
337	Constantine and Constans.	
340		Eusebius died.
354		Augustine born.
355		Themistius teaches at Constantinople.
360	Claudius Julian.	Sallust.
363	Jovian.	
364	Valentinian and Valens.	
379	Theodosius.	Eunapius.
380		Nemesius flourished.
384		Didymus of Alexandria. Jerome flourished.
391		Gregory Nazianzen.
394		Gregory Nyssen.
395	Arcadius and Honorius.	Division of the Roman Empire.
398		Ambrose died.
400		Nemesius died.
401		Plutarch, son of Nestor, flourished.

A.D.	*Greek Emperors.*	
402	Arcadius.	
408	Theodosius II.	
409		Macrobius. Pelagius.
410		Synesius.
412		Proclus born.
415		Death of Hypatia.
418		Pelagius condemned.
430		Augustine.
434		Syrianus flourished.
450	Marcian.	Hierocles. Olympiodorus flourished.
457	Leo I.	
470		Claudian of Messina flourished. Boëthius died.
474	Leo II. Zeno the Isaurian.	Marcian Capella flourished.
476	End of the Western Empire.	
480		Salvian. Cassiodorus born.
485		Proclus died. Succeeded by Marinus. Ammonius, son of Hermias.
487		Æneas of Gaza flourished.
490		Marinus died.
491	Anastasius.	Isidore succeeds Marinus.
518	Justin I.	
526		Boëthius beheaded.
527	Justinian.	
529		Philosophical schools formed at Athens.
533		Damascius returns from Persia with the Platonists. Philoponus flourished.
539		Cassiodorus shuts himself up in a cloister.
549		Damascius and Simplicius flourished.
563	Justinian II.	
575	Tiberius II.	Cassiodorus died.
582	Maurice.	
602	Phocas.	
604		Gregory the Great.
610	Heraclius.	
622		Flight of Mohammed.
636		Isidore of Seville died.
641	Constans III. and IV. Constantine II.	
668	Constans V.	
673		The Venerable Bede born.
685	Justin II.	
694	Leontius.	
698	Tiberius III.	

A.D.	*Greek Emperors.*	
711	Philippicus.	
713	Anastasius II.	
716	Theodosius III.	
717	Leo III., the Isaurian.	
735		Bede died.
736		Alcuinus born.
741	Constans VI.	
753	(Caliph Almanzor.)	
754		John of Damascus died.
776		Rhabanus Maurus born.
796	Irene.	
	German Emperors.	
800	Charlemagne. (HarounAlraschid.)	Alkendi flourished.
804		Alcuinus died.
814	Lewis the Pious.	
840	Lothaire.	
855	Lewis II.	
856		Rhabanus died.
875	Charles the Bald.	J. Scott Erigena comes to France.
877	Lewis III.	
879		Alfred the Great of England.
880	Charles the Fat.	
886		Erigena died.
887	Arnolph.	
891		Photius died.
899	Lewis IV.	
912	Conrad.	
919	Henry the Fowler.	
937	Otho the Great.	
954		Alfarabi died.
974	Otho II.	
980		Avicenna born.
987	Otho III.	
999		Pope Sylvester II.
1002	Henry II.	
1003		Sylvester II. died.
1020		Michael Psellus born.
1025	Conrad II.	
1034		Anselm born.
1036		Avicenna died.
1039	Henry III.	
1042		Lanfranc enters the convent of Bec.
1055		Hildebert of Lavardin born.
1056	Henry IV.	
1060		Anselm prior at Bec.
1072		Father Damien died. Al Gazel born.
1079		Abelard born.

A.D.	*German Emperors.*	
1080		Berenger of Tours died.
1089		Lanfranc archbishop of Canterbury.
1091		Bernard of Clairveaux born.
1092		Opinions of Roscellinus condemned at Soissons.
1096		Hugo St. Victor born.
1100		Michael Psellus died (or later).
		Eustachius of Nicea.
1107	Henry V.	
1109		Anselm archbishop of Canterbury.
1114		Alain de Lisle born.
1117		Anselm de Laon died.
1118		Abelard teaches at Paris.
1120		Abelard monk at St. Denis.
		William of Champeaux, bishop of Chalons, died.
1126	Lothaire.	
1127		Al Gazel died at Bagdad.
1134		Hildebert died.
1138	Conrad III.	
1139		Moses Maimonides born.
1140		Hugo St. Victor died.
1141		Gilbert Porretanus bishop of Poictiers.
1142		Abelard died.
1146		Ecclesiastical assemblies at Paris and Rheims against Gilbert Porretanus.
1150		Peter Lombard writes his Sentences.
1153	Frederic Barbarossa.	Bernard of Clairveaux died.
1154		Gilbert Porretanus died.
1164		Peter Lombard and Hugo of Amiens died.
1173		Richard St. Victor and Robert of Milan died.
1180		John of Salisbury died. Walter de St. Victor.
1190	Henry VI.	Tophäil died.
1193		Albert the Great born, according to some.
1198	Otho IV.	
1203		Alain de Lisle died.
1205		Maimonides and Peter of Poictiers died.
		Albert the Great born, according to others.
1206		Averroes died, according to some.
1209		David de Dinant. Amalric de Chartres died.
1214		Roger Bacon born.
1217		Averroes died, according to others.

A.D.	*German Emperors.*	
1217		Michael Scott at Toledo.
1218	Frederic II.	
1221		Bonaventura born.
1224		Thomas Aquinas born.
1234		Raymond Lully born.
1236		Albert the Great doctor of theology at Paris.
1245		Alexander of Hales.
1247		Thomas Aquinas goes to Paris. Ægidius Colonna born.
1248		William of Auvergne, bishop of Paris, died.
		Thomas Aquinas begins to teach according to the views of P. Lombard.
1250		Peter Albano born.
1251	Conrad IV	
1252		Foundation of the Sorbonne.
1253		Robert Greathead died.
1254		Nicephorus Blemmydas flourished.
1256		Thomas Aquinas doctor of theology.
1264		Vincent de Beauvais died.
1273	Rodolph I.	
1274		Thomas Aquinas died. Bonaventura died.
1275		J. Duns Scotus and Walter Burleigh born.
1277		John XXI., pope (Peter Hispanensis), died.
1280	Adolph of Nassau.	Albert the Great died.
1294	Albert I.	Roger Bacon died, according to some
1300		Richard of Middleton died.
1308	Henry VII.	Duns Scotus died.
1309		
1310		George Pachymeres died about this time.
1314	Lewis V.	
1315		Raymond Lully died.
		Francis Mayronis introduces the *Actus Sorbonnicus.*
1316		Ægidius Colonna died.
		Peter Albano died.
1322		Occam resists the pope.
1323		Harvay (Harvæus Natalis) died.
1325		Francis Mayronis died.
1330		Occam takes refuge with the Emperor Lewis.
1332		William Durand died.
		Theodore Metochyta died.
1337		Walter Burleigh died.
1343		Occam died.

A.D.	*German Emperors.*	
1346	Charles IV.	
1347		Occam died, according to others.
1349		Thomas de Bradwardyne and Robert Holkot died.
1350		Peter D'Ailly born.
1357		Thomas of Strasburg died.
1358		Buridan.
		Gregory of Rimini died.
1361		J. Tauler died.
1363		J. Gerson born.
1374		Petrarch born.
1379	Wenceslas.	
1382		Nicholas Oramus.
1388		Thomas à Kempis.
1395		Bessarion and George of Trebizond born.
1400	Robert.	
1401		Nicholas of Cusa born.
1408		Laurentius Valla born.
1410	Sigismund.	Matthew of Cracovia died.
1415		Emmanuel Chrysoloras died.
1419		J. Wessel Gansfort born.
1425		Peter D'Ailly died.
1429		J. Gerson died.
1430		Theodore Gaza in Italy.
1435		Marsilus Ficinus born.
1436		Raymond of Sebonde teaches at Tou louse.
1438	Albert II.	Gemisthius Pletho and Bessarion come to Florence.
1440	Frederic III.	Invention of Printing. Foundation of the Platonic Academy at Florence.
		Nicholas of Clemange died.
1443		Rodolph Agricola born.
1453	Taking of Constantinople.	
1455	Nicholas V.	Reuchlin born.
1457		Laurentius Valla died.
1462		Pomponatius born.
1463		John Picus Mirandola born.
1464		Nicholas of Cusa died.
		Cosmo de Medici and Pius II. died.
1467		Erasmus born.
1472		Bessarion died.
1473		Persecution of the Nominalists at Paris.
1478		Theodore Gaza died.
1480		Thomas More born.
1481		Francis Philelphus died.
1483		Paul Jovius born.

A.D.	*German Emperors.*	
1484		Julius Cæsar Scaliger born. LUTHER born.
1485		Rodolph Agricola died.
1486		J. Argyropulus and George Trebizond died, according to some.
1489		J. Wessel Gansfort died.
1492		Lorenzo de Medici died. Ludovicus Vives born.
1493	Maximilian I.	
		Theophrastus Paracelsus born.
		John Picus Mirandola died.
		Angelo Politian died.
1497		Melancthon born.
1499		Marsilus Ficinus died.
1500		Dominic of Flanders died.
1501		Jerome Cardan born.
1508		Bernardino Telesio born.
1509		Andrew Cæsalpini born.
1515		Peter Ramus born. Machiavelli flourished.
1517	(Beginning of the Reformation.)	
1519		
1520	Charles V.	
1522		Reuchlin died.
1525		Pomponatius died.
1527		Machiavelli died.
1529		Patrizzi born.
1533		John Francis Picus Mirandola slain.
		Montaigne born.
1535		Cornelius Agrippa died. Thomas More died.
1536		Erasmus died.
1537		J. Faber died.
1540		Ludovicus Vives died.
		Institution of the Jesuits
1541		Theophrastus Paracelsus died. Charron died.
1543		Copernicus died
1546		Augustine Niphus died (born 1473).
1547		James Sadolet died. Nicholas Taurellus and Justus Lipsius born.
1552		Paul Jovius died. Ces. Cremonini born.
1555		Simon Porta died.
1558	Ferdinand I.	
1560		Melancthon died.
1561		Francis Bacon born.
1562		Anthony Talon died. Francis Sanchez born.

A.D.	*German Emperors.*	
1564	Maximilian II.	
1568		Thomas Campanella born.
1569		
1572		Peter Ramus died. Dan. Sennert born.
		J. Sepulveda died.
1574		Robert Fludd born.
1575		Jacob Bœhme born.
1576	Rodolph II.	Jerome Cardan died.
1577		J. B. Van Helmont born.
1578		William Berigard born.
1580		Jordano Bruno leaves Italy.
1581		Lord Herbert of Cherbury born.
1583		Grotius born.
1586		Jacobus Schegk died. Lucilio Vanini and Le Vayer born.
1588		Telesio died. Thomas Hobbes born.
1589		James Zabarella died.
1592		Montaigne died.
		Gassendi born. Comnenus born.
1596		René Descartes born. J. Bodin died.
1597		Francis Patrizzi died.
1600		Jordano Bruno burned.
1603		Charron and Cæsalpini died.
1604		Francis Picolomini died.
1606		Nicholas Taurellus and Justus Lipsius died.
1614	Matthias.	Martin Schook born. Francis Suarez died.
		Fred. Merc. Van Helmont born.
1619	Ferdinand II.	Vanini burned.
1621		J. Barclay died.
1623		Blaise Pascal born.
1624		Jacob Bœhme died.
1625		Clauberg, Geulinx, and Wittich born
1626		Francis Bacon died.
1628		Ralph Goclenius died.
1630		Huet born. Cremonini died.
1632		Sanchez died
		Benedict Spinoza, John Locke, Sylvain Regis, Samuel Puffendorf, and Richard Cumberland born.
1634		P. Becker born.
1637	Ferdinand III.	Daniel Sennert and Robert Fludd
1638		died.
1639		Nicholas Malebranche born.
1642		Thomas Campanella died.
1644		Galileo died. Newton born.
1645		John Baptist Van Helmont died.
		Grotius died

A.D.	*German Emperors.*	
1646		Leibnitz born. Poiret born.
1647		Peter Bayle born.
1648		Herbert of Cherbury and Mersenne died.
1650		Descartes died.
1651		William de Tschirnhausen born.
1654		J. Selden died.
1655		Gassendi died. Christian Thomasius born.
1657	Leopold I.	
1659		Adrian Heerebord died. Wollaston born.
1662		Pascal died.
1663		Berigard died.
1665		J. Clauberg and M. Schock died.
1666		J. de Silhon died.
1669		Geulinx and J. Cocceius died.
1670		Sorbiere died.
1671		Comenius died. Shaftesbury born.
1672		La Mothe le Vayer died.
1675		Samuel Clarke born.
1677		Benedict Spinoza died. Thomas Gale, Francis Glisson, and Harrington died.
1679		Christian Wolff born. Hobbes died.
1680		Joseph Glanvill and La Rochefoucault died.
1684		Berkeley born. James Thomasius died.
1685		Lambert Velthuysen died.
1687		Henry More and Wittich died.
1688		Cudworth and Parker died.
1692		Bishop Butler born.
1694		Arnauld and Puffendorf died.
		Francis Hutcheson and Voltaire born.
1695		Nicole died.
1698		B. Becker and J. Pordage died.
1699		Frederic Merc. Van Helmont died.
1704		Locke and Bossuet died.
1705	Joseph I	J. Ray died. David Hartley born.
		Bayle died.
1707		Sylvain Regis died.
1708		Tschirnhausen and Jacquelot died.
1711		Hume born.
1712		Crusius and Rousseau born.
1713		Shaftesbury died.
1715		Malebranche died. Condillac and Helvetius born.
		Gellert born
1716		Leibnitz died.

A.D.	German Emperors.	
1718		Augustus Fardella died.
1719		Poiret and Richard Cumberland died
1720		Bonnet born.
1721		Huet died.
1722		Boulainvilliers died.
1723		Adam Smith born. Richard Price born.
1724		Wollaston died. Kant born. Ferguson born.
1727		Newton died.
1728		Christian Thomasius died.
1729		Samuel Clarke, Collins, and Buddæus died.
		Andrew Rüdiger died.
1731		Mandeville died.
1732		Erasmus Darwin born.
1733		W. Derham died. Joseph Priestley born.
1735		Le Clerc died. James Beattie born
1736	Charles VII.	
1740	Frederic II king of Prussia.	
1742		Garve born.
1743		Jacobi born. Paley born.
1744		John Baptist Vico and Joachim Lange died. Platner born.
1745	Francis I.	
1747		Francis Hutcheson died. Jeremy Bentham born
1748		Crousaz and Berlamaqui died.
1751		La Mettrie died.
1752		Hansch died. Bishop Butler died.
1753		Dugald Stewart born. De Maistre born.
1754		Berkeley and Christian Wolff died.
		Destutt de Tracy born.
1755		Montesquieu died. Volney born.
1756		Laromiguière born.
1757		David Hartley died. Cabanis born.
1758		Gall born.
1759		Maupertius died. Reinhold born.
1762		Alex. Baumgarten died. Fichte born.
1764		Massias born
1765	Joseph II.	Reimarus died. Sir James Mackintosh born.
1766		Thomas Abbt and Gotsched died.
1768		Bouterwek born. Azais born. Maine de Biran born. Royer-Collard born.
1769		Gellert died. Keratry born.
1770		Winckler, D'Argens, and Formey died. Hegel born.

A.D.	*German Emperors.*	
1771		Helvetius died.
1772		Cramer died. Coleridge born.
1774		Quesnay died.
1775		Crusius and Walsch died. Schelling born.
1776		Hume died. Ballanche born.
1777		Meyer and Lambert died. Dr. Thomas Brown born.
1778		Voltaire and Rousseau died.
1779		Sulzer died.
1780		Condillac and Batteux died. De Lamenais born.
1781		Ernesti and Lessing died.
1782		Henry Home and Iselin died.
1783		D'Alembert died.
1784		Diderot died.
1785		Beaumeister and Mably died.
1786		Mendelsohn died.
1788		Hamann and Filangieri died.
1789	French Revolution.	
1790	Leopold II.	Adam Smith, Fr. Hemsterhuys, and Basedow died.
1791		Richard Price, Daries, and Nettelbladt died.
		Victor Cousin born.
1792	Francis II.	
1793		Bonnet, Moritz, Beccaria, and Condorcet died.
		Berard born.
1796		Thomas Reid died. Theodore Jouffroy born.
1798		Garve died.
1800		Maimon died.
1801		Heidenreich and Darwin died.
1802		Engel died
1803		James Beattie and Herder died.
1804		Kant, Joseph Priestley, and St. Martin died.
1805		Paley died.
1806		Tiedemann died.
1808		Bardili died. Cabanis died.
1809		J. A. Eberhardt and Steinbart died.
1812		Christian E. Schmidt died.
1813		J. A. H. Ulrich died.
1814		Fichte died.
1816		Ferguson died.
1817		De Dalberg died.
1818		Platner and Campe died.
1819		Jacobi and Solger died.
1820		Wyttenbach and Klein died.

A.D.	*German Emperors.*	
1820		Dr. Thomas Brown died.
		Volney died.
1821		Feder and Buhle died.
		De Maistre died.
1822		Eschenmayer died.
1823		Reinhold and Maass died.
1824		Maine de Biran died.
1828		Dugald Stewart died.
		Bouterwek died
		Gall died.
		Berard died.
1831		Hegel died.
1832		Jeremy Bentham died.
		Sir James Mackintosh died.
1834		Coleridge died.

THE END.

www.ingramcontent.com/pod-product-compliance
Lightning Source LLC
LaVergne TN
LVHW010230110826
845151LV00004B/1250
* 9 7 8 1 4 2 5 5 2 5 4 5 3 *